This Way Forward

Sermons That Matter

Tom Evans

Parson's Porch Books

www.parsonsporchbooks.com

This Way Forward: Sermon That Matters

ISBN: Softcover 978-1-951472-39-9

Copyright © 2020 by Tom Evans

All rights reserved. No part of this book may be reproduced or transmitted in any form or by any means, electronic or mechanical, including photocopying, recording, or by any information storage and retrieval system, without permission in writing from the publisher.

This Way Forward

Contents

About Sermons Matters 7

Ordinary Saints … In Friendship 9
    Mark 2:4

Ordinary Saints … In Generosity 15
    Romans 16:1-2

Ordinary Saints … in Prayer 21
    Acts 10:1-16, 34,35

Ordinary Saints … in Suffering 27
    Mark 15:21

Ordinary Saints … And the Impossible 33
    Mark 16:1-11

Does God Still Speak To Us? 39
    Job 38:1; Hebrews 1:1-2

Why Do the Good Die Young? 46
    Romans 14:8

Where Are The Wonders? 53
    Psalm 44:1-3: 23-26

WHY Did You Do It? 59
    John 3:16

What Does God Think Of Doubters? 66
    Matthew 14: 22-33

Finding Peace: In the Bible 73
  Philippians 4:4-9
Finding Peace…with the Past…through Forgiveness 79
  Romans 5:1-5
Finding Peace…In The Present…Through Contentment 86
  1 Timothy 6:6-8
Finding Peace… in the Future…. through Faith 94
  John 16:31-33
500 Years Of Reformation: Sola Scriptura 101
  2 Timothy 3:15-17
500 Years Of Reformation: Sola Fide 107
  Romans 3:21-22
500 Years Of Reformation: Sola Gratia 115
  Romans 3:23-24
500 Years Of Reformation: Solus Christus 121
  Acts 4:12
Awkward Verses… An Eye for An Eye 126
  Matthew 5:38-42; Exodus 21:22-24
Awkward Verses… Women Should Have Authority Over Their Head 133
  1 Corinthians 11
Awkward Verses… Give Up or Drop Dead 142
  Acts 5:1-6

About *Sermons Matters*

Parson's Porch Books is delighted to present to you this series called *Sermons Matter*.

We believe that many of the best writers are pastors who take the role of preacher seriously. Week in, and week out, they exegete scripture, research material, write and deliver sermons in the context of the life of their particular congregation in their given community.

We further believe that sermons are extensions of Holy Scripture which need to be published beyond the manuscripts which are written for delivery each Sunday. Books serve as a vehicle for the sermon to continue to proclaim the Good News of the Morning to a broader audience.

In this volume, **Tom Evans** gives us a concert of sermons which challenges the one who *read*s him preach to examine one's heart, mind and soul.

We celebrate the wonderful occasion of the preaching event in Christian worship when the Pastor speaks, the People listen and the Work of the Church proceeds.

Take, Read, and Heed.

David Russell Tullock, M.Div., D.Min.
Publisher | Parson's Porch Books

Ordinary Saints ... In Friendship
Mark 2:4

This Lent we are going to explore those characters in the Bible who don't take up more than a sentence or two, perhaps we don't even learn their name but, nevertheless, they made it into scripture. They are in and out in a verse but, when it was their time, they did the Lord's will. Their acts were not extraordinary. In fact, they simply did the ordinary things you or I might do on any given day.

Through this series I hope that each of us might gain a better understanding of what it means to be a saint in the kingdom of God. It does not mean we are especially holy people. It does not mean we have extraordinary virtue or stamina. It means we have a holy God and, though maybe a simple one, we have a holy calling – to be of service to our God whenever we can, in whatever manner we are asked.

We shall discover it happens in the ordinary moments of life – by carrying someone's burden a little way down the road, using your money to further a cause, helping a sick friend to get the care they need.

These are the simple acts of human kindness that have become a part of God's Holy Word and that I suspect most of you do every day of your life and, when you do them in God's name, you are a saint.

Today we discover what it takes to be an ordinary saint in friendship. The Bible tells us four people carried a sick man. We don't know their names. They are never mentioned again and yet, a simple bold act of friendship leads to healing, to forgiveness, and to the glory of God.

Their first thought was straightforward. Bring their sick friend to Jesus. There were no ambulances, so carrying him was the only way. Friendship begins with effort.

> "Friendship is unnecessary, like philosophy, like art.... It has no survival value; rather it is one of those things which give value to survival." — C.S. Lewis, The Four Loves

A friend is someone you are not obligated to help out of some quid-pro-quo arrangement or because they are family, but you want to because ... well ... they're your friend. I know many of you have taken friends to doctor's appointments or sat with them for hours in the hospital, simply to let them know you care.

> When we honestly ask ourselves which person in our lives mean the most to us, we often find that it is those who, instead of giving advice, solutions, or cures, have chosen rather to share our pain and touch our wounds with a warm and tender hand. The friend who can be silent with us in a moment of despair or confusion, who can stay with us in an hour of grief and bereavement, who can tolerate not knowing, not curing, not healing and face with us the reality of our powerlessness, that is a friend who cares.
>
> — Henri J.M. Nouwen,

And a friend who cares is willing to go a layer deeper. A true friend does not give up at the first sign of trouble. Undeterred by the crowd blocking their path to Jesus, they go to the roof, cut a hole in it, and lower him. Cutting a hole in a roof!?

A true friend is willing to be a fool, risk stares and even scorn. You have seen such simple but bold acts before. Not too long ago, a high school student was stricken with cancer and, of course, the chemo made his hair fall out. So, what do friends do? They shaved their heads, unashamed to be different if it meant helping their friend!

It helped him get through the treatments and he said, "It makes me feel loved, makes me feel special, feel good that I go to school here and have all these friends to help me out."

> *Piglet sidled up to Pooh from behind.*
>
> *"Pooh!" he whispered.*
>
> *"Yes, Piglet?"*
>
> *"Nothing," said Piglet, taking Pooh's paw. "I just wanted to be sure of you."*
>
> — A.A. Milne, <u>The House at Pooh Corner</u>

Simply knowing a friend is nearby can make all the difference. At least it did for Piglet.

But what turns this story into something more than a simple lesson in friendship and turns this talk into a sermon, of course, is the presence of God in the person of Jesus.

Perhaps these four friends simply thought they were carrying this man to a healer, a person of renowned, who could help with their friend's illness.

So Jesus thought to himself as this man suddenly was thrust before him. W.W.I.D! What would I (Jesus) do in this instance?

If you or I had Jesus' power, we would have healed him, of course! But that is not what Jesus did! At least not a first. In fact, he seems to balk at the act of healing.

This man was brought to be healed of his physical infirmity. They thought to do him an amazing kindness, but a temporary one, nonetheless. Someday this man would become sick again and, as we all will, die. But when a friend carries another to Christ, it leads to miracles we cannot imagine.

Jesus looks at the man and declares, "Your sins are forgiven!" Hearing words of forgiveness can be a source of great healing. But I imagine when you hear them from our Lord himself, it is an entirely unique moment. In hearing Jesus speak forgiveness two things happen.

First, you suddenly become aware of precisely how far you are from being what God made you to be. Your power to repress your own faults and foibles disappears. You become aware of just how rotten your own sins truly are and that your harsh judgements on others' sins are overblown. You realize that you had a gargantuan log in your own eye, as you decried the speck in others. You know that Jesus knows you, truly knows you better than you know yourself.

But that lasts only for an instant.

Secondly, and more importantly, when Jesus speaks these words of forgiveness you believe it, like you never have before. You can tell he truly means it. There is no holding back. There is no, "I forgive you, if…." All your sins you suddenly become aware of, leave your body like a tumor cut from your soul.

Knowing the value of things beyond physical healing led Hellen Keller to say, "I would rather walk with a friend in the dark, than alone in the light." Friends can change your life.

But there is more to this story. There is so much more.

The power of friends becomes the power of saints when acted upon in the name of God. Take another look at the story. Mark tells us when Jesus saw THEIR faith!!! The friends' faith, not the man's! Normally we think forgiveness comes from repentance; but that is not what happens here; he did not judge the man's heart. The man did not ask for forgiveness and, frankly, neither did the friends.

And yet somehow, through the simple, bold kindness of friends it happens. Something divine and eternal arises out of their good intentions. An encounter they never conceived, a blessing none of them imagined! That is what happens when God and friendship collides!

After some squabbling with the Pharisees, Jesus does heal the man. Less for the man's sake and more as Jesus says, "so that you may know that the Son of Man has authority on earth to forgive sins."

But the story is not finished. Not only is the man healed of his physical infirmity and cleansed of the soul sickness, all the crowd experiences the presence of God.

For being a witness to the friends' courage and Jesus' divine action leads them to be knocked off their feet to glorify God and declare, "We have never seen anything like this!"

Indeed, I bet they never had. But that is what happens when ordinary saints are bold friends in the name of Jesus. Amen!

Ordinary Saints … In Generosity
Romans 16:1-2

As we continue our Lenten series on ordinary saints this week we turn to the women. There are scores of women who have become a part of the story of salvation because of their generosity at critical moments.

There was Lydia the dealer in purple cloth who opened her home to the apostles, whose biblical story only lasts two verses! And yet she was the beginning of spreading the gospel beyond its birthplace. She was the very first European convert!

In Luke 8, we learn of three women Mary Magdalene, Joanna, and Susanna, who had been all been healed, who in turn provided for the apostles out of their resources. There is Phoebe from Romans 16 whom Paul commends to be welcomed as a saint who was a benefactor of many including Paul himself.

Some of these women were people of significant financial means but others simply had an extra room, an extra plate, and a willingness to use it to God's glory.

These women, as are all those we are exploring this Lent, at first glance appear to be a mere footnote in the biblical story. These people are you and me, normal everyday people, who fade in the background in the face of tempestuous and loquacious Paul, in the face of supremely courageous and beautiful Esther, or stubborn rock like Peter.

The funny, or rather curious thing about the Bible, is that those who are mentioned as being financial supporters are almost all women!!!

Napoleon once said, "An army marches on its stomach!" This means you cannot march an army any further than you can feed them. Think about it. It's the reason the Confederates took the paths North they did. Once the Union Army choked off supply lines from the coast, they went inland through apple orchards to find food along the way.

The same was true for spreading the gospel of Jesus Christ. The apostle's needed places to sleep; they needed clothes; they needed food and water. Without the Lydia's and Phoebe's, the gospel never would have made it past a single day's travel! It never would have reached beyond Israel and you and I would not be here today! That means the ordinary saints are just as crucial as Paul, Peter, Mary and more.

An ordinary saint in generosity is someone who believes in the cause, who wants to be a part of the story but may not have the time or the particular skill to otherwise be of assistance. Giving generously allows you to be a part of something whether you can participate directly or not.

The gift, no matter your means, is also a way of not sitting on the sidelines even when you know your gift is not the dollar that will make it happen. You know in your heart (and God knows as well!) that you are doing your part and not simply riding on the coattails of the faithfulness of others.

But it's not all about money.

The key attribute of an ordinary saint is seen in Phoebe. Paul uses the word *prostasis* meaning patroness, to describe her. The word literally means "to stand alongside of." An ordinary saint stands by someone in need by offering what they have, be it money, time, or a spare room.

According to one source *prostasis*

> is [a] classical Greek [word] describing a trainer in the Olympic games, who stood by the athletes to see that they were properly trained and not over-trained and rightly girded when they lined up for the signal.

So this financial assistance is not only about the cause, but perhaps even more about the person, about supporting someone who is doing the Lord's work. Ordinary generosity becomes the act of an ordinary saint, a *prostasis*, when it is done to support those in the Lord's work.

Your generous gift is a way of saying, "I believe in you!" to those on the frontlines of ministry. This is so clear in our work in Haiti. This past January I saw the powerful results in the first school building we helped build. Yes, there were dozens of smiling children studying and learning. But I also saw how our generosity gave strength, courage, and hope to Madame Jackie and the teachers to keep going when things get so impossibly difficult. The building gives them the space they need but through our generosity helps them to feel God is with them.

That is why every gift counts, no matter the size.

Of course there are other ways to stand alongside of someone in addition to monetary gifts. Thus Lydia is lauded for opening up her home. Open homes and open hearts. It takes all of us being generous with what we have to further the kingdom of God in this world.

I remember visiting one member during my time as a pastor in Magnolia, Arkansas, Margaret Skinner. She was a widow whose children lived out of town. She had no one to dote upon so during our monthly visits she would treat me to a hot cup of coffee, a freshly baked bran muffin (which I can still taste!) Not being able to get around much she wanted to know how she could be of use. As I took a bite of that muffin, I knew exactly how she could serve as an ordinary saint! Bake those muffins for those who had experienced loss as she had. Soon scores of people were tasting the blessing of her love. By the way I also almost killed her, not on purpose mind you! Seven years after we had left Arkansas my daughter, Liz and I went back to visit the church and Ms. Margaret. She had moved into a nursing home, so I went to surprise her. As soon as I walked in and said "Hello", she clutched her heart with a stunned look on her face! But thankfully only for a moment! She almost died of a heart attack right then! I almost made an ordinary saint into an ordinary angel!

Anyone can be an ordinary saint. It does not matter the age. You remember that story I told months ago about the child whose friend had cancer. He wrote a book called *Chocolate Bar* that raise one million dollars to help find a cure. God gives each of us something we can use to stand alongside others working for our Lord's purposes.

This Way Forward

Your generosity is amazing. Many of you know last year we exceed our operating income by over $100,000! But did you also know that you gave an additional $500,000 beyond the budget for mission to support Winter Warmth, the DR, Mobile Meals for Cast for Saint Luke's and much more!!

By living as an ordinary saint extraordinary things happen by the power of God. One of the most impactful of all acts was performed by a mail carrier for Christ!

According to the Tyndale Bulletin in ancient Rome there were three ways mail was delivered.

> The only postal service, the *cursus publicus*, was meant solely for the transmission of official material. The well-to-do often used a *tabellarius*, a slave who acted as a courier. For the great majority, however, personal correspondence had to be entrusted to anyone— often a complete stranger—who was heading for the right destination or even just in the right direction.

Many of you know that Paul longed to get to Rome to spread the gospel there but for various reasons his travels took him elsewhere. It just might be that preventing him from going to Rome was the Lord's intent so that this letter would be written. But since Paul could not go, he needed someone he trusted to take it there. Surely not some random stranger.

Paul chose Phoebe. The woman who stood alongside him and others, through her generosity, was given one of the most sacred tasks in the history of the church. Paul must have had tremendous respect for her because the letter carrier would do more than deliver a piece of paper. She would serve as Paul's presence to the Romans. She would help explain the letter's purpose and Paul's passion.

She hardly could have known the profound impact this letter would have throughout the entire planet. She could not have known Paul's powerful elegance in describing the righteousness of God through the faith of Jesus Christ would become Martin Luther's inspiration to launch the Protestant Reformation.

An ordinary saint was given a simple task to carry a letter the results of which literally changed the world. Let's take a moment to learn about another ordinary saint who reminds us that being generous with our time in caring for others is something everyone should be doing. Amen.

Ordinary Saints ... in Prayer
Acts 10:1-16, 34,35

In the book of Acts, Luke shares with us another story of an ordinary saint in the person of a Roman guard named Cornelius. He was not someone of grand plans or schemes. He simply followed an internal compass that both opened his wallet to the poor and his soul to God in prayer. Luke tells us he was a 'God fearer', which meant he was drawn to Judaism but had not converted; In his time Gandhi could have been considered as such with Christianity for he had respect and honor for Jesus but remained a Hindu at heart.

This generous caring soldier not being a Jew makes me wonder. If this story took place today who would he be? A Hindu? Buddhist? Muslim? Would we have the same trouble accepting him that Peter did? After all God had to send Peter a vision and even then, it took several tries to convince Peter to open wide his heart. It is all too easy to cast someone as our enemy but when in their hearts you can see they have the same internal compass their particular affiliations melt away before us.

We can scarcely appreciate the stunning reality of Cornelius' story. He was a Roman soldier, an enemy of Jews and its new sect the Christians. He worked on the side of the empire, (for Lord Vader so to speak) which sought to suppress the Christians, to hunt them down and kill them. Yet, Peter and the Lord accepted him.

Something drew him to the word of God. Perhaps the truth of

it spoke to some part of him that his training had not wiped from his soul. Something deep in the recesses of his being that knew it rang true. So he hungered to know more of this God.

Cornelius counts as an Ordinary Saint this Lent because it is the everyday decision of doing what is right that makes a saint, not grand acts of heroism.

An ordinary saint has a genuine heart...

...that leads to prayer

   ...which bears fruit in compassionate action

      ...while breaking down barriers.

I know you know many people like Cornelius with a heart of gold. Perhaps one is coming to mind right now. They never think of themselves; they don't complain; they do what is right, and they respect other people even if they don't agree. They are not at the center of things. At parties they recede into the background and you would not know they are there if you didn't bump into them.

These are the ones doing precisely what the Lord requires of them; the ones who know to do justice, love kindness, and to walk humbly. Even if they don't know the words, they know it inside their hearts.

Their genuine heart leads to authentic prayer.

A seeking soul led Cornelius to pray to this God he did not know. Perhaps like you and I he saw so much in his world that needed changing. Perhaps he was tired of seeing the horrible plight of the poor, the endless war and the religious persecution that he himself was a part of. Perhaps he didn't know what else to do so he looked to the God of the Jews.

When ordinary saints say their prayers it's with true compassion for all people whether they think, look, or act like them. The compassion is not bound by race, political party, or religion, and they are drawn to scriptural truths that are open to people of all religions: love God and love neighbor; do unto others; visit those in prison, extend hospitality.

But the ordinary saint does not stop with prayer. The prayers spur one to act. Cornelius was also a man of compassionate action. Simple but compassionate. Undoubtedly his prayers opened his heart even wider to the plight of the poor. Without any social safety net, it was far worse for those in his time to be without means, so Cornelius regularly gave alms to fill hungry stomachs.

An ordinary saint daily does what the Lord asks without self-pity or self-congratulations.

I knew a person in Magnolia who took care of her husband's failing health for 20 years, then daily took care of her mother for the next 20 until her mother died at 101. Forty years she did this.

Her name was Newlene Van Frank and each day she served the Lord's will through serving others. She brought no attention to herself and did not bemoan her plight. These are the people that inspire me, that give me hope about the world;

their lives shout louder than any dour newscast can, that in fact people are doing good in this world.

The heart, the prayers, and the acts all break down barriers, the barriers between us and God and the barriers between one person and another.

And so even though Cornelius did not yet truly know God, God knew him. God saw this man's faithfulness and reached out.

If you find yourself lost in theology or doctrine, like you are just not quite sure of your belief, don't worry you are not lost to God. If doubts are weighing you down and your belief is slipping like water through your fingers don't lose hope.

Reach out in prayer. Reach out in acts of love and God will find you like He did Cornelius.

Like the aroma of fragrant offerings his prayers ascended and pleased God. To God it smelled like sweet devotion. God's passions know no political party, nationality or even religion. He seeks those with right heart and right actions.

Once again, an ordinary saint changes the world. Up to this point the gospel was only for the chosen. And we can see in Peter how hard it was to conceive beyond this fact. But God chose Cornelius an enemy of the faith to be the very first non-Jew to receive the good news of the gospel. Cornelius was not looking to shake the world, or to be recognized; rather it was this daily faithfulness that led God to choose him for this honor.

So when the barrier between us and God dissolves it enables us to connect to others, even those of different races, religions and economics.

A few Saturday's ago I enjoyed a delicious breakfast with the Transparent Men Bible study group. It is an intentionally interracial group of men who come together for breakfast once a month for fellowship, study, and prayer. Piper, a regular attender and breakfast cooker shared a story he had a few months ago at our downtown coffee shop.

He was sitting at one of the outside tables along with a few other people when what appeared to be a homeless man came walking by. The man stopped at the first table and asked for some change and was refused. He went to the next table with the same result. He took one look at Piper decided it wasn't worth the effort and kept on walking. At that point Piper was interested in knowing more so he called to the man and said "Why not me? Maybe I can help." He explained he had recently been released from prison and came to Spartanburg because he had heard it was a generous town. Though he had trouble finding a place to stay his few days here changed his life.

As you all know anybody released from prison generally does not have the means to support themselves upon release and oftentimes their family ties have been severed for one reason or another, so they must rely on the kindness of strangers to carry them through at least for a few days, perhaps a few weeks.

He said to Piper, "I have been a racist all my life. Born and raised that way, but no more. Begging isn't easy. You get so many looks. But since I came here every single black person that I have asked for some spare change has been kind and generous to me. I am no longer going to hate."

Part of the task of the ordinary saint is to treat all people whatever their background and belief as people who deserve empathy, respect, and kindness and to offer it in Jesus's name. Like Cornelius those people who gave to this man out of the kindness of their hearts changed a life but perhaps not in the way they intended. They opened a man's heart to accept his brother's and sister's whom he had judged and rejected all his life.

A genuine seeking heart centered in prayer that spurs compassionate action leads to the breaking down of barriers- that is the calling card of an ordinary saint. Won't you be one to! Amen.

Ordinary Saints ... in Suffering
Mark 15:21

Scholarly research believes Simon was an African Jew, since his hometown of Cyrene is in modern Libya, in the north of Africa. He is among the more well-known ordinary saints we are exploring through this series. Today the Catholic's annually remember Simon's role in the fifth of the Stations of the Cross. There may also have been veneration of his and his ancestor's bones as an ossuary was found in 1941, dated at around AD 70, found in territory belonging to Cyrene Jews, with the inscription, "Alexander son of Simon." Today there is a Cyrenian movement in England and Ireland dedicated to sharing the burden of others.

Nevertheless, his story only takes up a single verse. The Bible tells us,

> *They compelled a passer-by, who was coming in from the country, to carry his cross; it was Simon of Cyrene, the father of Alexander and Rufus.*

That is all we know of Simon; everything the Bible has to tell us; no great feat of strength; no profound act of courage. Jesus calls all of us to take up our cross daily and follow him. Our cross is a unique burden that life thrusts upon us.

And yet like in this passage the cross we carry more often than not is carrying the burden of another a little way down the road. This is more than helping someone through a difficult task. It is feeling the weight of their burden so that for a time theirs is lighter.

It is letting their pain become yours.

An article from the Catholic Review entitled, *Afrocentric, Lessons from Simon of Cyrene,* offers a critical insight.

> The significance of the story of Simon of Cyrene is that the most important crosses that we will bear in our lives belong to someone else. Thus, how well we bear our personal crosses, whether of our own making or an accident of birth, is much less of a story than how well we carry the crosses of family, friends and perhaps most importantly, the crosses of strangers.

"The most important cross we bear in this life belongs to someone else." Bearing our own cross helps us triumph through adversity and builds character and fortitude.

Hellen Keller carried the cross of being deaf and blind with exceptional courage which shaped her into an American hero.

But, Anne Sullivan, her teacher and companion was the ordinary saint who helped bear Keller's burden enabling Keller to become an inspiration for us all, just as Simon helped Jesus when he carried his cross.

For the most part carrying another's cross only brings us pain and suffering. But if we have the compassion of Christ within us like him, we may not be eager, but we will be willing.

This is why the modern movement named after Simon...

> ... has as its guiding principle "sharing the burden" ...[through] providing services to homeless and other disadvantaged groups in society...

Serving the homeless does not further our life's goals. It is not easy or glamorous. It means working with people oftentimes, whose problems have accumulated over a lifetime that will not be fixed in one, or perhaps even in one hundred evenings. But carrying that cross even for a brief time can ease their pain.

I remember working with the people without homes in New York City. The man who ran the 'Midnight Run' meal ministry was formerly homeless. He had his Irish shillelagh, basically a walking stick, which he waved in our faces telling us if he would bash our head in if we came at him wrong. We laughed nervously but we could see he actually meant it. He looked as ancient as the myths of old, grizzled and curmudgeonly, a caricature truly if I ever saw one; feisty, but he shared the burden.

He did it because he knew how hard it was. He shared his own story of lost opportunities, of failed marriages, estranged children, and deep psychosis. But instead of running as far away from that painful time as he could he went back to the streets to carry their cross as well as he was able. Going back to those streets meant revisiting painful even terrifying times, but he knew others were lost in the dark and he was going to do whatever he could to shine a little light.

So he brought food to fill their stomachs. Toiletry products to give them some dignity. And he brought along youth groups and young people to meet them to remind them of better times and to see that in this world there are still those with a bright-eyed look at life, who are filled with hope for the future. I could see in their eyes that those few moments with young people were intoxicating and gave them great solace and comfort. But I could also see the pain it cost our host. I saw him more than once reflexively wave his Irish Shillelagh at passersby. Perhaps he was remembering those times he had been attacked on the streets.

Being an ordinary saint in suffering is not as freeing or joyful as being generous with our time and money or rewarding as being a friend. It costs us.

And yet there is a personal payoff. It makes us more aware of our own burdens. It makes us feel more essentially human. It makes us more like Christ.

To care for someone during a severe illness is to know them warts and all. It is a time when they are deeply vulnerable, to wipe their brow, mop their vomit, change their bedpan, bathe them with a sponge it all requires carrying their burden and a willingness to utterly put aside your own needs for a time. Paul tells us to carry another's burden is to fulfill the law of Christ. The law of Christ is of course love, so to carry another's burden is the essence of love and love is what God made us for. That is what makes carrying another's burden a deep privilege.

Robert Lanborn professor of pastoral theology in England and an MD, said "he only is whole who shares in the brokenness of others."

That is the theology of the cross. It is the essence of our salvation. In that act of sacrifice, Jesus bore the pain and sin of the whole world and when a Roman soldier saw his manner of death he declared "Truly this was man was God's son." Jesus of Nazareth came to be seen as the Son of God through his death on a cross. God became visible in the act of sharing another's pain.

And so I can scarcely imagine what these few moments were like for Simon. The Bible teaches us that at times God feels deep pain and anguish over the evil we do. No fool Cornelius didn't volunteer, the Bible tells he was forced and yet, like no one else in all of history he carried God's burden for a time; the weight of it all is so tremendous even God feels it. To feel another's pain is a deeply intimate act. It can show us the essence of who they are. To know what causes another pain is to know their heart, to know their mind. It shows us what is important to them. It is to know the essence of their humanity. And so Simon came to know God in a way that no one else has.

Though Simon carried a cruel burden for Jesus for a time, we look back and see it as a great honor; in some ways greater than any other- to relieve the suffering of God for a few paces. I imagine that moment changed him forever.

Simon of Cyrene: After James Wright by Madeline Fentress:

> *I saw the spears, the cross, the crown of jest. Behind, a shove—I fell out from the crowd.*
> *I felt the press of wood against my chest.*
> *Beneath his yoke, I bore the weight; too proud*
> *To hold the gaze that came from eyes of ash, Though days ago, I stood with palm leaves strewn. My help was like the morning's missing lash:*

This Way Forward

He had to live to see the afternoon.
Now every day I wake and walk that hill again. The dust, the sun,
the thorns, the ache of stones— The details freshly resurrected when
Once at the top, I sit among the bones—
The wine and gall, the dice, the final cry.
I tasted death with him, then watched him die.

Ordinary Saints ... And the Impossible
Mark 16:1-11

Jesus Christ is risen today, Alleluia! We sing these joyous words every Easter and it thrills us to hear the trumpets, the choir, and to see a full church. It is a heartening moment filling us with confidence and positive energy.

However, in the midst of the beautiful lilies, new dresses, and Easter brunches it can be easy for the message to get lost and forget why we are here.

Easter makes the impossible our destiny.

On that Saturday morning so long ago all the people whom Jesus touched in his life once again woke up. They woke up back to reality, a reality that for a brief time Jesus brushed away. They woke up into a world in which true and lasting change was proven impossible just as it is every day for us. But on this day, it stung harder.

Their dear friend Jesus was dead. But Jesus was more than their friend. He was their hope. Their hope that Rome would be thrown off their backs. Their hope of being truly accepted by others. Their hope that their daughter would live. That their friend would walk. Their hope that enemies could become friends. Their hope that they would discover and know the very meaning of life.

Reality stung a bit harder on that morning because a small kernel in their heart actually believed for a moment that there was something more to this Jesus.

This Way Forward

So on the next day Mary Magdalene had resigned herself once again to life as usual. The life of dashed dreams but still, she would do what was right. She would go and honor her friend with the proper rituals.

And that's when it happened. The impossible is now the inevitable. Jesus was alive! Mary Magdalene was so overwhelmed she ran in terrified amazement! And so should we. Because we are just like her. People too afraid to truly hope, to crestfallen to truly believe

She was one of the Ordinary Saints we studied this past Lent. Though all these saints appeared only for a verse or two their impact was profound. They were men and women no different than you or I ready to do what they could but also filled with fears and foibles, so If we understand their lives, we understand our own.

I propose that we spend some time this morning exploring what Jesus' resurrection would have meant for them and so in turn remind ourselves of just how earth shatteringly spectacular this event is for you, me, indeed the entire planet.

In Paul's letter to the Romans we learned about Phoebe. She was an ordinary saint who had been blessed with financial means and she used them to great effect to support God's work. Although money can do many things Phoebe would have also known its limitations. Phoebe could make the world a better place through her generosity but there were vastly more problems than her money could fix. Being a woman of power she would have known that in spite of the control she had there were far greater things in this life it could not touch.

That's perhaps why she carried Paul's letter to the Romans. She discovered in those pages the promise of something more.

We live in a world which money motivates and moves a great deal. But she knew it was impossible for it to create love; it cannot prevent addictions; it cannot stop death. In Jesus' resurrection she would have discovered something of a deeper power than she had even seen before: the power of God's love. As Paul described in the letter, she was carrying to Rome it is a love which conquers all things! Through that resurrection she would have seen that there is no problem so big and scary that God does not have the power to fix it.

Cornelius, the roman soldier, was another ordinary saint. He worked to keep order in the world through violence and supported an evil regime-the Roman Empire. He knew of God; He knew of faithfulness and duty. But he knew he needed more. He could see that the law of "might makes right" does not make sense. He knew it was impossible for war to create true peace. In discovering the resurrection, he would come to know the most powerful being in the universe chose the path of self-sacrifice, chose to heal the world not through the exercise of brute strength but of servanthood. He came to know it is not might of the sword but only the power of love and grace that can create true freedom.

Simon of Cyrene was the saint who carried the cross of Christ a few steps down the road. He had seen sheer hatred. He saw it was impossible for mere humility and service to defeat evil, for he saw how evil could snuff a life at a mere whim. His soul must have been seared to be so close to such an awful thing. Many of you have been bruised by tragic death, addiction, violence. But in the resurrection Simon would have come to see that God can defeat all things; that love does conquer all; and that there is nothing that God will not forgive, not even the killing of His only son. He would now know that nothing can separate us from the love of God in Christ Jesus our Lord.

Four people who brought their lame friend to Jesus were our first set of ordinary saints. You remember, they dug a hole in a stranger's roof to avoid the crowd so they could get to Jesus. Though he healed his friend they knew it was impossible for this healing to last beyond a few years.

Virtually all of us have taken a friend or relative to the hospital at one time or another and when they became better it filled us with joy. Perhaps it's because we only truly appreciate health in the face of sickness. It is only in times of illness that we know wholeness.

In 1988, while training for a triathlon a truck plowed into John Maclean, fracturing his ribs, sternum, breaking his back and turning him into a paraplegic. He went from being a professional rugby player to being confined to a wheelchair for 25 years. Of course he felt sorry for himself many times and whenever he did, he recalled something that happened about a year before he was injured.

While training on a rainy day he made some polite conversation with an older woman saying, "It's not a very nice day is it." She turned around looked him in the eye and said, "Young man, it's a beautiful day. It's another day I'm alive."

During those decades of sitting in that wheelchair he came to truly appreciate that woman's words.

Yet, God had in mind something more.

We all know that technology is progressing at a fantastic rate. What was impossible 25 years ago is routine today. The pipe dream he dared not wish too hard for, lest he sink into despair, became real. The words Jesus spoke to that lame man so long ago became real for John Maclean, "Stand up and walk", the doctor said.

And he did. Haltingly and with the aid of technology. Nevertheless, he walked. And he walked far enough to finish that triathlon he started a lifetime ago.

Nothing. Nothing! Nothing!!! is impossible.

To see him on YouTube to learn to walk is like watching a toddler discover their own legs for the first time.

He was reborn to speak. It was in injury John discovered what wholeness is, not just in body, but in mind and in spirit.

Those people who brought their friend to Jesus only received temporary reprieve for him. His body would break down again. It would decay and die, death claims us all and it can make the joy of healing seem bittersweet, that we are given something so wonderful only to have it taken away for good, forever.

But I imagine when those friends heard of Jesus' resurrection, to see and know God's power of life over death is to receive the promise of being re-born, not simply to walk again but into something greater than we can ever know in this life. Jesus resurrection is God's promise that nothing is impossible! The resurrection is the promise for all our friends that our parting from each other in this life is only a temporary affliction that nothing not even death can stand against the power and righteousness of God, the power of God to reconcile the whole world. In the resurrection the impossible becomes our destiny and all "ordinary saints" discover extraordinary joy! Amen.

Does God Still Speak to Us?
Job 38:1; Hebrews 1:1-2

In the Bible, God speaks in "many and various ways" as Hebrews tell us. God speaks through angels, like with Mary. God speaks through bizarre writing on the wall, as with Daniel. God speaks through burning bushes, as to Moses, and God even speaks directly, in an audible voice, like with Samuel.

We envy those days in which God communicated so clearly and we want to know if (or rather how) God still speaks today. I propose this morning we explore biblical examples of God's communication, Angels, direct, audible speech, and "out of the whirlwind".

Angels

In the Bible, God makes somewhat regular use of fantastic creatures to speak to us. In Revelation these angels have six wings, can fly, and perpetually declare God's truth. At Jesus' resurrection, angels speak words of comfort to Mary. But does God still send these angels today?

Many Christians believe that God sends them special messengers to give them comfort, guidance, and direction. It may be a chance encounter with a stranger, who offers a kind word. And, since "angel" means messenger, perhaps we can conclude that yes, God does still speak to us through angels.

But if by angels we are referring to these 6-winged beings that live with God, are not human, and come down to earth to convey his truth, I am not so sure. It simply does not reflect how I have experienced God or the world in general. There are no stories I have heard that are compelling. I must admit that there is a measure of skepticism in my 21st century mind.

But I am not the only one. In fact, it is the Bible that tells us to be careful. We should be careful to not too quickly believe somebody's claim that an angel spoke to them. In Colossians, Paul says, "Do not let anyone who delights in false humility and the worship of angels disqualify you. Such a person also goes into great detail about what they have seen; they are puffed up with idle notions by their unspiritual mind."

The apostle Paul, who saw a fantastic and incredible vision when Christ struck him blind on the road to Damascus, he's the one who doubts angels have visited other people.

Does God speak to us in a voice we can hear?

Curiously enough, even in the Bible, which is literally God's word to us, God speaking to us, if you will, there is a lot about the absence of God's word. There are moments in which God not only seemed silent, but God was silent. In the book of Samuel, we are told, "Now the boy Samuel was ministering to the Lord under Eli. The word of the Lord was rare in those days; visions were not widespread."

So, when Samuel was lying down in the temple near the Ark and he heard a voice call his name, he assumed it was Eli. He went to Eli only to discover he hadn't called him. This happens two more times and, finally, Eli catches on that God is calling Samuel, so Eli tells Samuel, "Go, lie down; and if he calls you, you shall say, 'Speak, Lord, for your servant is listening.'"

Even though this story is about God speaking, we are first told that this is a rare occurrence. It was so unexpected that neither Samuel nor Eli knew it was God. But that was in Biblical times. What about today?

There's an old joke: When you talk to God, we call it prayer, but when God talks to you, we call it schizophrenia.

While we can accept that God spoke in days of old, we have a much harder time believing it today. We have a hard time believing because we have seen so many instances throughout history of people claiming, with utter certainty, that God has spoken to them, leading to profound abuse of power and great tragedy.

People understandably want to be open to the idea that God still speaks directly and clearly to individuals. But it is precisely that kind of openness to someone else's direct line to God that enables a madman like Jim Jones to convince people that God wants them to drink Kool-Aid laced with cyanide!

Out of the Whirlwind

Then... how does God communicate with us?

For this answer we turn to Job. As you recall, Job had been afflicted by disease, by the death of his loved ones, and then, even further, by his friends!

For several chapters his friends try to teach Job what it is that God is saying – they are shortsighted, pedantic, and trivial thoughts. His friends speak with utter confidence and conviction. Then his friends turn those thoughts and they turn those beliefs towards Job, to condemn him.

Perhaps one of the greatest ills of our time is that we have all become like Job's friends. It seems that everyone is claiming to know what God wants, what God thinks, what God has to say. While at the same time, with supposed good intentions, explaining to everyone who does not think like they do why they are sinners and why they are suffering God's wrath.

It is the reason I cannot stand watching the news. There is no humility. No respect. No willingness to actually listen, to listen from that broken frail part of ourselves. But they all keep shouting and condemning each other, claiming absolute certainty. Paul lamented such certainty, and Jim Jones exposed its dangers.

But Job is different from his friends. And it is his suffering that has done this.

Job, like you and me, desperately wanted to know exactly what God thinks. Job wanted the handwriting on the wall, so to speak – or the message from an angel – to know what to do, to know what to believe, to know why his life was so hard.

And, to truly get a feel for Job's aching, yearning, desire to hear God's word, you have to sit down and read this book all in one sitting. Only then can you get a full sense of the existential crisis that Job was experiencing - - and how impossibly hard it was for him to not be given a direct word - - and how horribly frustrating it was for him to have his friends presume to know exactly what it was that Job had done wrong.

Job's frustration builds and builds, chapter after chapter. That building is a metaphor of our lives, years and decades that we yearn to know what it is that God has to say to us, yearning for God to speak to us directly, and, only at that point of utter exhaustion...

God's presence erupts onto the scene!

The Bible tells us, "Out of the whirlwind God spoke!"

Essentially, God says, "I am God, you are not. There are things in this world that have nothing to do with you, that you will never understand."

After listening to God's extensive speech about the divine power to create, to destroy, to control the winds and the seas and the creatures of the earth, Job completely and utterly admits that he had tried to speak for God rather than hear what God had to say.

Job seems to finally realize that the only way to hear and to know God's will is utter openness, complete humility, and an unrestrained desire to hear what God is saying, without inserting the smallest bit of his own will and his own thoughts.

And though Job is never given an answer to his questions there is something profound that happens, because Job was finally ready to truly listen – and it changed everything.

It changed something within Job; it opened his heart.

And, instead of Job focusing on his suffering, his loss, and his lack of understanding, Job goes to God in prayer – not for himself but – to ask God to be merciful and forgive those that had blamed him, condemned him, and shamed him.

In his humility before God, Job's heart was turned away from himself to those who opposed him.

And that is when the miracle happens. In Job 42:10: "The Lord restored his fortune when he prayed for his friends."

Job is healed of his affliction, Job finds peace, Job finds family, and not only does Job receive restoration and the joy of life, but Job's friends receive God's mercy as well.

So does God speak to us today?

Yes, unequivocally, yes! God speaks in more powerful and profound and spectacular ways than we can possibly imagine! God speaks to us in the whirlwind! God speaks to us in the chaotic unpredictable moments of life!

But Scripture teaches us that it won't be easy to hear; it almost assuredly will not come to us through an angel; it almost assuredly will not come to us through an audible voice, but it will come. It will come, only the Lord knows how, but when it does, it will knock you flat!

And it can change everything. It changed Job's world and it can change ours.

His heart of humility, his profound desire to hear what God had to say, led to the healing of his community.

If we can all have that same courage to listen and to love those who oppose us, it can change ours as well.

Why Do the Good Die Young?
Romans 14:8

When I first conceived of this sermon series, I thought it might be a good break from the lectionary and an opportunity, during the summer, to engage in some lighter material. I imagined you might pose some curious questions that would be fun for all of us to dive in together.

But, very quickly, I found the questions you wanted addressed were right at the very heart of our faith and some of your deepest struggles in life.

Today we will deal with perhaps the most difficult and personally challenging question that you have asked, and that people of faith have struggled with for millennia:

Why do the good die young?

It is a question as old as humanity itself. It grows from an internal sense that there is something wrong with the world. That suffering and death are not meant to be a part of this life. That we were created for something greater than a few decades of a mixture of happiness, grief, joy, and loss.

Even so when somebody has lived a full life there is a sense of completeness. When that loved one passed from this life to the next, we find comfort in our grief.

But, when people are taken early in life, before they can even experience the full measure of what this brief existence has to offer, it feels like the universe has cheated them. It seems to us that the very least an all-powerful and all-loving God could do for us would be a guarantee of sorts – a guarantee that every person gets to live out a certain measure of what we might call *a full life*.

There are four boys in my family but there is a fifth child, a daughter, Rachel. Rachel died when she was only a few days old. Some 51 years later, I still want to know what Rachel is like. I still feel cheated. I want to know how her presence would have made growing up in a household with four boys different. As a teenager I wanted to know silly things like, "Would she have helped me meet cute girls in high school?"

"Why do the good die young" is question that has led to many different answers. Such unjust deaths erode our sense of God's justice and power. In fact, Billy Joel's song, *"Only the good die young"* centers around this problem. The song is trying to convince a young lady to engage in carnal activities. The justification is that chastity does not matter because God can't exist, since the good die young all the time!

In the face of this question, even Biblical authors have been utterly confounded. The author of Ecclesiastes simply threw his hands up and said, "It's all vanity" (Ecclesiastes 1:2). So, to propose that we're going to spend a few minutes this morning and come up with the answer is, in itself, an exercise in naïveté. I also want to make it clear that I don't think there is a single right answer to this question; to fully explore, even the biblical thoughts, would take us years.

Having said that, by the end of the sermon we will have an answer to our question. It is an answer that at times might bring you great comfort and at other times might leave you frustrated and confused. For this answer we turn to the story of Lazarus.

We all know that the shortest verse in the Bible is one of the most powerful. When Jesus saw all the grief from Lazarus' death, he wept (John 11:35). Jesus was touched by their sorrow and, so, he raised Lazarus from the dead. Whether or not we ever obtain what we feel is a satisfactory answer to our question, we can gain comfort that Jesus cares.

An implicit assumption within our question is that the person who dies young has been cheated out of the blessings of a full life. And, that if God was appropriately acting godly, some dramatic action would be taken – such as in the Lazarus story.

However, in rereading this passage, a question occurred to me. Did Jesus raise Lazarus from the dead out of compassion for Lazarus? - or for his loved ones? In other words, did Lazarus' early death rob him of some essential experience that Jesus wanted to restore for him? - or was Jesus motivated by something else?

If it was to help Lazarus, then we are forced to ask ourselves "Why did Jesus delay?" A detail that John specifically points out, showing that he shares our frustration, as did Lazarus's sisters, who both went to Jesus saying, "If you had been here, he would not have died."

Their questions reflect the same sentiment our question does today, "God, why do you let the good die young?!"

Jesus' rationale does not offer much comfort. In fact, it may add to our frustration.

It is clear Jesus intended to delay so that Lazarus would suffer death, and, in turn, he could raise him from the dead, leading people to believe in his power. Jesus says precisely this to the disciples. The "illness is for God's glory, so that the Son of God might be glorified through it." (John 11:4)

Never once does the Gospel of John, or Jesus' words, ever indicate that the raising of Lazarus was meant to benefit Lazarus himself. Rather, it was done to demonstrate Jesus' power over death and out of compassion for those who loved Lazarus. Jesus weeps when he sees the grief of the crowd, not upon hearing of Lazarus' death. Thus, our assumption that God's solution, to those good people who suffer an early death, should be a longer life is cast into doubt. In fact, under certain conditions, Isaiah claims the opposite!

It's a rather shocking statement that has to do with the events taking place at the time. It was a time of war, a time of tragedy, a time of treachery, and a time of great loss for the people of Israel. Isaiah declares, "the devout are taken away and nobody understands." (Isaiah 57:1) Just like today, when the good die young, we simply don't understand it. But Isaiah continues "for the righteous are taken away from calamity and they enter into peace." (Isaiah 57:1-2) Isaiah is suggesting that these righteous people were better off to be taken early, rather than to endure all the calamites Israel was facing.

We must be very careful. Isaiah's thoughts are not meant to be a universal answer to our question. We know that, at times,

God explicitly keeps servants to endure suffering and challenge in order to accomplish his purposes. We know Paul yearned to go be with God in heaven, but God delayed so that Paul could continue his ministry. The example in Isaiah 57 claims that God has other purposes in mind than simply making this world the best it can be for everyone. God has greater aims than we have for ourselves.

It's true the Bible makes it clear that death is not a part of God's original plan for us or for creation. Paul tells us death is the enemy. In fact, that it is the final enemy. But Paul also tells us, and if we believe it then his answer matters, that God has conquered this death; that Jesus has defeated it. That it no longer has any sting to it.

When I was nine years old, I contracted a disease called septic arthritis. It took three different hospitals to figure out what was wrong with me. Still today, I don't know much about the disease, but I do know – at least from what I was told – is that it is an infection that if it continues to go through your body, it can not only devastate you, but it can kill you. After the third hospital figured out what was wrong with me, they were getting ready to put me in an ambulance to a fourth hospital to take me to surgery – immediately. As my mother was filling out the hospital's surgical release form, she got to the part that releases the hospital from any liability "in case of patient's death". She hesitated. Then she learned that there was a surgeon on the other end – at the fourth hospital – that understood this disease and had successfully treated this disease. Everyone that my mother knew at the Georgetown Medical Center had tremendous confidence in that surgeon. Even though she didn't know what was going to happen during the surgery, even though I would be completely unaware of what was going on, she signed that piece of paper because she trusted that the surgeon was going to take care of me. The sting of the fear that my mother was experiencing was taken away.

That's why, in the 14th chapter of Romans, the Apostle Paul writes, "*If we live, we live for the Lord; and if we die, we die for the Lord. So, whether we live or die, we belong to the Lord.*"

That is the Bible's answer to our question.

"God, why do the good die young? Why do you allow that to happen?"

"Because, though it may not seem it to you, (and I understand that) whether you live or whether you die, you are in my hands."

For those of us who live, God is saying, "I am with you."

God realizes that, even though death no longer has any eternal sting, there is still that sting of loss. That tragic loss means that we will never get to live out our days with our beloved spouse, that we will never get to raise that precious child into adulthood, that we will never get to see what our only sister was like.

For those of us that are left behind, God is saying, "I understand your fear. I understand your sense of loss and I send you the Holy Spirit to be your comforter and your strength. But, even more, I send you hope. Because I promise, in ways you cannot understand, that I am with your loved ones every step of the way, they too are in my hands. I promise, as I did in the Psalms, that when they pass through the valley of the shadow of death, they need not fear. And I promise, as I did in Isaiah, that when they pass through the waters, and the fires, I am with them."

God is telling us that he is with our loved ones, as he promised in the Psalms, when they go through this final stage from here to the next life – when they walk through the valley of the shadow of death – they need not have any fear.

Ultimately, God's answer to the tragedy of an early death is not a longer life here, but a new life. A new body, a life in the heavens with God where there is no more pain and no more sorrow. Where death is no more! Where we need no longer fear for our loved one. Where we can be assured, they are in the best hands possible. They are at peace.

That is the good news of the gospel! That Jesus Christ has risen! And that his life gives us life eternal.

Thanks be to God.

Where Are the Wonders?
Psalm 44:1-3: 23-26

"Rouse yourself! Why do you sleep O Lord?" That was the frustrated phrase the psalmist used. He remembered hearing fantastic stories of God's powerful interventions to defeat Israel's foes. Those were the days! God leveled armies, parted seas, brought down the wall of Jericho. Those were the days when God was God!

This morning, we are exploring God's apparent refusal to get too involved in today's politics and world problems. The Old Testament is filled with deeds of great power – Wonders as they are known by – because they overwhelm us in both scope and sheer audacity. Like Psalm 44, we would like this same intervention.

Now, I am not talking about those healing miracles. Many of us believe these types of miracles still happen every day, if less fantastically, than they did in Jesus' time. I am talking about the acts of God, which literally stopped the sun! That would surely get people's attention!

Certainly, there are those who still see such mighty acts from God in today's world. These interpretations include attributing hurricanes, earthquakes, or just about any natural disaster, to God's divine wrath for sins they find especially heinous. Besides making God seem especially cruel (and judgmental), it seems to me God, in Jesus Christ, showed us that God's greater anger is kindled against precisely the type of self-righteous judgement these so-called evangelists are engaging in. As a result, more often than not, it is their interpretation that makes us believe even less in such dramatic acts, rather than more.

And yet, if God is the same today, as yesterday, and will be tomorrow, it seems problematic to dismiss such miracles of nature out of hand. In fact, I believe that God does act "wonderfully" and those who experience them have a responsibility to share their stories.

In Psalm 44, it is obvious people had done so. In verse one we read, "We have heard with our ears what our ancestors told us." Those stories became a part of his faith. Even if we don't experience it directly, God wants us to know about them. In fact, the Hebrew law requires sharing God's great miracles. Deuteronomy 6:20 says,

> ... you shall say to your children, 'We were Pharaoh's slaves in Egypt, but the Lord brought us out of Egypt with a mighty hand. The Lord displayed before our eyes great and awesome signs and wonders...

As we can see the primary reason for these wonders was liberation, not wanton violence, from a frustrated God. That is what the psalmist is asking, for God to give them relief from their enemies who have hemmed them in all around.

But it feels, to us, as if God has backed off from being that same God we read about in the Bible. It feels as if that is the type of God we need now more than ever. But, Psalm 44 makes it clear people in those days felt the same way.

The Bible is filled with God's great acts, but it is filled, even more, with people's frustration. Not every chapter in the Bible is a miracle. Even then they were rare. In Psalm 44 we are told he heard of these stories from his ancestors. Implying that it had been at least several generations since such bold acts had been seen.

Far from God sleeping on the job, as the Psalmist accused, the divine plan turns a different way. Even though we are more concerned with God's acts of power, God was always more concerned something else.

This life is a supreme gift from God. It is a glorious bounty. God wants everyone to experience this bounty. God wants justice executed and that right swiftly. But there is something God wants even more – trust and a new heart.

It is hard for us to imagine that God, remaining hidden, is worth all the trouble it causes. That all the wars, all the famine, all the hatred, all the indifference could be taken care of if God just performed some fantastic spectacle. If God made the divine presence known, in a way for which there could be no room for doubt, surely people would be more obedient.

But this is not what God is looking for – belief that stems from proof. God wants the type of belief that comes from not seeing.

> "We walk by faith and not by sight." (2 Corinthians 5:7)

> "Faith is the conviction of things NOT seen." (Hebrews 11:1)

God wants that part of us that connects to our soul to believe, not only our mind. For if we believed, simply because our head knew God was real, because it had been proved to us, then that most important part of ourselves might never make that leap. To believe without sight requires reaching out – with a "sixth sense" of sorts.

Imagine, for a moment, you are trapped in a warehouse that is flooding. You're not too worried because, despite the many obstacles you must traverse, you can see your way out. But then, suddenly, the electricity goes out. Panic and fear set in. You begin making your way out, but you're constantly smashing your shins and walking into walls. You realize that you have been wandering for 15 minutes and you know you have made a dramatically wrong turn, because the exit was only about 20 yards away. And the water continues to rise. And then you hear a voice. It is your friend who can see you. They begin to tell you when to turn left, when to stop, and when to lift your leg to step over an obstacle. At first, you're somewhat frustrated because you're still running into walls and you're still smashing your foot. It's because you're not used to being led by something other than your own eyes; you're not used to truly listening to someone else. But, as time goes by, you get better at trusting this voice and soon find your way to safety.

To walk by faith and not by sight is to trust. To follow God, from the very depths of our being, takes hard work. It takes a lot of bumps and bruises and, at times, we will feel as if we are walking blindly. But God keeps us blind, so to speak, to train us to seek him out with our soul. So, while our heads might more readily agree and listen to God should we see some spectacular sight that proves divine power, that deeper part of ourselves which seeks our own rules and our own path would never let go and fully trust.

Which leads to God's second reason to refrain from fantastic acts of power and rescue. God has made us in the image of God. And God wants us to act like it. God is molding us like a piece of clay; and that molding has to do with making us into people of divine intentions. By remaining hidden, God forces us to explore our own motivations.

If God were constantly revealing the divine self, then we might be more likely to put money in the offering plate, we might be more willing to speak words of kindness, we might refrain from abusing the planet, and we might stop from engaging in war. But God did not create human beings to be mere shadow puppets, two-dimensional images forced to imitate God's actions, like those shadows cast upon the wall.

This, I think, is the method that God wants us to use to forge the world into the type of world God intends it to be. Yes, we need just laws; yes, we need law enforcement; but, without this change of heart we will be perpetually chasing our tail and never catch it. Because if we only change the laws, but don't change within, people will continue to find new ways to hate, new ways to rob, new ways to discriminate.

God wants a deep change to take place in each of us, which cannot happen should God constantly use these fantastic means to accomplish the divine will. God wants us to do it! That's why we are made as we are, not mere animals, but with a soul. That's what a soul is!

A new and right heart with us. A new heart within us all. That is God's primary aim for us in this life. At times, God will allow life to be impossibly difficult and unfair in order to not compromise this goal.

Just this past week, you may have heard about the terrible story of an elderly, Mexican man, 91 years old, who was in this country visiting some family. He was beaten with a brick. He was told to "go back home". What do you think his response was to this terrible act? What would *your* response be? I know what mine would be – "send them to jail!" But, he said, "I don't resent them. May God forgive them." Now, *that* is acting like our Lord.

God wants us to believe in what God believes in. God us wants to be agents of hope, justice, and love. God wants us to be fully realized "little lower than God(s)" (Psalm 8).

God remains hidden because God wants us act like God - even if he didn't exist. Amen.

WHY Did You Do It?
John 3:16

This morning's question came from a member as a heartfelt yearning to know: "Why did you do this for us? Why did you send Jesus? What did you see in us?"

The subtext of this question is both a feeling that we aren't worthy, but even more a realization that we know we are not worth it. We don't feel worthy because we haven't laid sufficient groundwork with our actions, with our thoughts, with our devotion, that might lead God to take such actions. But, even more, we know we're not worth it; that we are never ever going to make up for everything that God had to go through to bring us the gift of salvation. Jesus' R.O.I. (return on investment) for saving humanity will always be deep in the red.

So, the question "Why did you do this for us?" takes hold of two emotions within us, simultaneously. First, profound gratitude, gratitude that God was willing to do this for us even though, clearly, we don't deserve it. It's something like bringing a coupon to a restaurant for a buy-one-get-one-free entrée and, as you are handing it to the waiter, you realize it is expired. You don't deserve the discount, but you desperately want the discount, and the waiter gives it to you! You are filled with joy!

But, secondly, there is almost a sense of resentment within it. A sense that we are now going to have to try to live up to something that we're not ready to dive into.

This is like when you terribly fouled up your saxophone recital. Despite feeling embarrassed, you also felt a sigh of relief. You were sure your mother wouldn't make you take these lessons anymore and you were looking forward to the chance of spending more time playing soccer with your friends!

…But alas *my* mom (okay we are really talking about me here) graciously gave me one more chance – a chance that I really didn't want.

When God saved us, God also made it clear that we would have to work very hard to live into this new life we have been given.

Now that we understand this question contains divergent emotions within us, let's begin to answer it. In one sense, the answer to this question is easy. God did it because God loves us, because God is love. But, on the other hand, that answer doesn't get us anywhere, because it just takes us to the next question "Why in the world did you love us?"

There are plenty of verses in scripture that disclose our confusion and our unease with God's choice of us.

Peter said to Jesus (it's always Peter isn't it?),

How often should I forgive…seven times?

Sounds reasonable! Sounds generous! Sounds like a lot! How many people have you forgiven seven times?!

[But] Jesus said to him,

'Not seven times, but I tell you, seventy-seven times. (Matthew 18:21b-22)

Peter asks Jesus this question because he suspects that Jesus has an entirely different approach than anyone else, he has ever met. Not only because we don't want to get burned, time and time again, from people taking advantage of us (which is certainly understandable) but because we have come to believe that sometimes tough love is necessary. Furthermore, Peter knows, because he knows it himself, that people don't want to be forgiven that many times because it just adds to the burden of guilt.

As difficult as endless forgiveness is for us to fathom, God's love goes another layer deeper into sacrificing for those who have been forgiven.

Indeed, rarely will anyone die for a righteous person – though perhaps for a good person someone might actually dare to die. But God proves his love for us in that while we still were sinners Christ died for us. (Romans 5:7)

We love things in appropriate measure. For our mother, our dear friend, our child, we would do most anything. But San Francisco Police Officer, Anna Cuthbertson, listened to a podcast (a podcast!) and decided to donate her kidney to a complete stranger, 65-year-old Joan Grealis. Officer Cuthbertson now has only one kidney. She has put her own life in jeopardy for someone who means nothing to her.

But Paul is not talking about strangers. Paul is telling us that Christ's sacrifice was for sinners, like donating both your kidneys to a serial arsonist. It simply does not make sense to make such a sacrifice for people like us.

But God's love goes even further.

But I say to you who hear, Love your enemies, do good to those who hate you. (Matthew 5:44)

Has anything more radical ever been said in the history of the world.

In the 1990s, Amy Biehl was a young American woman volunteering in South Africa as it emerged from the terror of Apartheid. Amy was brutally murdered when a mob ripped her from her car as she was driving a friend to the impoverished Gugulethu Township.

Amy's parents created a foundation to continue her work in Cape Town, giving opportunities to youth from troubled communities.

Their willingness to become involved in their daughter's place of murder was surprising in and of itself. But their love went to the level that Jesus called for when Amy's parents endorsed her murderers' application for amnesty through South Africa's Truth and Reconciliation Commission. Could you imagine signing such a piece of paper! And, yet, they took Jesus' words to love your enemies even one step further when they hired one of them to work at the foundation named in her memory. Could you imagine working side-by-side with your child's murder?...

Clearly, we don't always want this love from God because, in turn, we will expect to offer the same to others.

And, so, the more I consider this question "Why did you do this for us God?" The more...the more...the more...confused I am.

To say that Christ did this for us – that Christ left heaven, left paradise, left the eternal praise of the angels, to come down to earth, to become human with aches and with pains, with exhaustion, flu, hard work – that Christ came knowingly, to endure not only all these normal problems but also came to endure rejection by his hometown, scorn from his family, abandonment from his friends, and execution by his people and the government, – to say Christ went through all of this out of love – in some ways just adds to our confusion. Because to love sinners (really love them), to love enemies (to truly sacrifice *for them*), and to love those who never seem willing to learn and to do better (to truly forgive them again and again, again, and again, and again, and again, and again, and again, and again... (I'm going to say this 490 times!) and again, and again, and again, and again, and again, and again, again and again, again, and again, and again, and again, and again, and again, and again, and again, and again, and again, and again, and again, and again...

It is absolutely unbelievable.

We have to ask this question, "Why did you do this for us?" Because Jesus' love is NOTHING like ours.

it truly has NO CONDITIONS.

it is ABSOLUTE AND TOTAL

it is a SHEER AND UTTER GIFT.

Why did God do this for us. Why did God love us?

Because divine love has no conditions. Which means God is going to love us no matter what we do, meaning we do not have to perform to a certain level. If we were a pet dog, God would continue to love us no matter how many times we soiled the divine carpet.

Furthermore, there are no conditions that require us to please God in order to continue to be loved. We could be the most wretched, mangy, ugly, boring, stupid dog ever to walk the face of the earth and God would continue to love us, to really love us.

That's what divine love is.

Why did God do this for us? Why does God love us?

Because divine love is complete, which means God loves every part of who we are. And God doesn't just love every part of who we are, but divine love loves us with the full power and passion of the Trinity. Even though we might be a dog, God loves us with the same passion, with the same level of engagement and commitment and power, as God loves one of the angels in heaven.

That's what divine love is.

Why did God do this for us? Why does God love us?

Because divine love is complete and an utter gift. You sometimes might hear that salvation is something like a door that needs to be opened. Hogwash! Unbiblical nonsense. God smashes through the door to get to us. We don't need faith in order to receive this gift. If we were that doggie in the window, waiting to be adopted by a passerby, it is not as if God is choosing that dog with the greatest puppy-dog eyes, that looks at us longingly, to please come and rescue me – No!

We could be that dog asleep, as he passed by. We could be the dog barking madly at everyone and everything around us. We could be the dog that tries the bite His hand – and God would still rescue us.

Because that is what divine love is.

I don't get it.

Amen.

What Does God Think of Doubters?
Matthew 14: 22-33

When the question, "What does God think of doubters" was asked, I immediately became enthusiastic. Several people leaped into my brain – Moses, Peter, Sarah, Joseph – all interesting characters that could make for fascinating exploration.

But as I began to prepare for this sermon, I must confess I got somewhat nervous. I myself have had considerable doubts over the course of the years. And there are certain aspects of the faith that still trouble me.

Furthermore, I realized that those passages I could easily recall were all of a single mindset. They all served to bolster my own position. As I began to dig a little bit deeper into Scripture, the picture wasn't quite as simple as I thought at first.

It also quickly became clear that God does not have a single point of view when it comes to doubters. So, rather than trying to emerge with one particular answer this morning, we will explore several passages to gain a better understanding on the Biblical point of view of doubt and, hopefully in the process, a well-rounded perspective on our own sometimes-stumbling faith.

Perhaps it should go without saying, but God prefers that we have faith rather than doubt. But evidently the Bible thought it needed saying because in Hebrews we read,

This Way Forward

And without faith it is impossible to please him, for whoever would draw near to God must believe that he exists… (Hebrew 11:6)

Faith is not only for our own benefit; our belief pleases God. It is clear that, at times, God becomes quite frustrated with our lack of trust. It kindles God's anger against the people of Israel. God has presented you and me with creation as evidence of power and planted the Holy Spirit within us that confirms his existence. Yet, we still doubt.

Peter's doubt exasperated Jesus. He performed miracles in front of the disciples and they still hesitated to fully commit themselves.

When Moses went up the mountain to be with God, it did not take long for the people to devolve into doubt which morphed into idol worship. Remember they erected a golden calf and credited it with liberating them from Egypt. God was furious!

This incident reveals the true danger of doubt. As humans we will always worship *something*, whether it's success, sex, or power.

In our doubt we can be easily led to abandon our morals, to seek personal gain at the expense of others. It is lack of faith in God that enables the Enron's of the world to bilk hard-working people out of millions. It is lack of faith in God that has enabled us to treat God's creation as a personal sewer dump at various times in history.

In the face of doubt, God will take firm action. You remember Zechariah? Upon seeing an ANGEL speak of the coming birth of his Son, he asks for proof. Here was the angel Gabriel's response,

> *.. you will be silent and unable to speak until the day that these things take place, because you did not believe my words...* (Luke 1:18-20)

God will reprimand doubters and train them into faith. God did not take away either the call of Israel or the promised child to Zechariah because of their doubt. But God did discipline them.

When I was a young boy, on Sunday afternoons, we would often go to my grandparents' house for Sunday lunch. Grandma made the most amazing roast beef! The slow-cooked carrots were the only vegetable I would ever eat! and I've still, to this day, never tasted gravy quite as good. (sorry mom!)

But since there were four boys fighting to sop up the last bit of gravy with her homemade bread, occasionally we caused a bit of a ruckus... knocked over a chair or two and maybe a lamp, might have even used some language that didn't suit the Sunday afternoon meal.

Discipline meant the dreaded Deacon's bench. Grandma Rian would sit me down, look me straight in the eye while leaning over, and pointing her finger at my face instructed me to consider the error of my ways or something of the sort.

I would sit there for what seemed like a full hour – absolutely bored out of my skull. That was, in fact, the worst part of the punishment.

I can't imagine now that it was actually that long. But as the minutes ticked by, eventually my mind turned to the precipitating event.

Granted, I spent most of the time fuming that it was my brother's fault, not mine, while concocting various means of revenge. And, yet, eventually, there was always a part of me that did contemplate my sin. Even saying it now, it sounds so archaic. And upon reflection, that punishment, that discipline, I believe has made me a better person today.

Zechariah's punishment was somewhat similar. He was forced to be silent, rather than a Deacons' bench, he would have silence unto himself. This would make him completely unable to invent any rationalizations or excuses to those around him, thereby forcing him to struggle internally with everything that happened.

But, having faith rather than doubt is not simply about pleasing God.

And Jesus answered them, "Truly, I say to you, if you have faith and do not doubt, …even if you say to this mountain, 'Be taken up and thrown into the sea,' it will happen. (Matthew 21:21)

Now I am not sure it is as simple as that… Yes, I guess I am doubting the word of my Lord…

It is clear, faith by its very nature is empowering. There is a tremendous difference on the golf course when I believe I can hit the drive and when I don't. The former will lead to many pleasant outcomes, the latter to a day of drudgery, sifting through the forest to find my ball. That belief in myself allows me to access the gifts God has given me as meager as they may be.

If belief in my own gifts makes for a better day on the golf course, imagine what belief in the power of God can unlock.

If you believe Jesus, it gives power to move mountains.

It is not so much that God sits back waiting for us to acknowledge him and then extends a blessing to us, as it is that faith is the critical component to receive God's outstretched hand.

And though doubt frustrates God, God can still work with it. This is crucial to understanding that there is productive doubt as well as doubt that devolves into idolatry.

In fact, God prefers doubt to two other alternatives – disbelief and indifference.

Disbelief is different than doubt. The person who doubts still has a part of themselves connected to God. The person who doubts is wrestling with God. The person who disbelieves has completely abandoned any sense that God exists. And indifference, the mirror image of disbelief, God finds even more troublesome.

This Way Forward

The indifferent person, like those who disbelieve completely, fails to engage God or act upon Godly principles. You remember God's anger in Revelation at the church in Laodicea? God says, "because you are lukewarm, neither cold nor hot, I am going to spit you out of my mouth!"

I think those who worshipped the golden calf did so not out of doubt of the existence of God, as they didn't want to be troubled with the hard parts of faith.

They didn't want to bother reaching out to God within their hearts; they wanted it to be easy and so they made a golden calf, a god that they could see and make their own.

They knew the golden calf wouldn't tell them to do things they didn't want to do. So, perhaps, it was not so much doubt they were experiencing as it was the reality that they didn't really care about God. They were indifferent to the Lordship of God.

The disbeliever and the indifferent both fail to connect to God.

Contrast this with Peter's actions. The disciples see Jesus walking toward them while they're in the middle of a lake. Though they are all afraid, Peter is the only one with enough courage to speak. As he is walking toward Jesus on the water, the wind and the waves suddenly shake his faith. But though his faith is shaken, he cries out not just to the wind but to Jesus, "Lord save me!"

And therein lies the key.

Peter, though he doubts clearly, is not lukewarm and God can work with that! And so…

> *Jesus immediately reached out his hand and took hold of him, saying to him, "O you of little faith, why did you doubt?"* (Matthew 14:31)

When he sees Jesus walk on the water, a part of him wants to believe. So, even in doubt, he takes that bold move to step out onto the water when nobody else would. Yes, Peter has doubt. Yes, Peter begins to sink because of his doubt.

But because Peter had enough faith to step out of that boat…

…he was the only one of the disciples to walk on water.

…he was the only one to feel the hand of the Lord lift him up.

Yes, God can work with doubt. God can work with your doubt, but doubt that is active, not doubt that sits on its hands but doubt that takes those faltering first steps toward him.

I don't think Jesus' response to Peter was a reprimand, but rather an expression of longing on Jesus' part. He longed for Peter's faith to be fully strong because he knew that Peter was going to need it.

When you doubt that God is at work, when you doubt that God cares – challenge God; cry out to God. When your faith is faltering, take that step, that first step toward God…and you too will feel the hand of the Lord lift you up.

What does God think of doubters like Peter, doubters like us?

God loves them.

Amen.

Finding Peace: In the Bible
Philippians 4:4-9

This month we will be chasing the ever-elusive goal of peace. We will be looking through a Biblical lens to learn:

> ... how to have peace with our past through not holding the mistakes of our youth against us and not harboring resentment for those who did us wrong, in a word... forgiveness;

> ... how to have peace with the present through accepting the blessings we do have while learning not to constantly grasping for more, in a word ...contentment; and

> ... how to have peace with the future through a clear-eyed understanding that history is in the hands of God and that His power is sufficient, in a word... faith.

Striving for peace is a deeply Biblical endeavor. In the King James version of scripture, the word appears 429 times! The more things change the more they stay the same. Peace will always be on the top of humanity's needs and the Bible tells us how to find it!

Paul devotes a lot to talking of peace because he knew, more than most, what it was to be at war...

> ...at war with himself, the ever-present demon of temptation in the side of his flesh;

...at war with his past, his murderous actions against his fellow Jews that professed Christ;

...at war with his kin, his fellow converts who rejected his authority;

...at war with the government, though a citizen of Rome, they imprisoned him, beat him, and ultimately killed him.

But, in Philippians, Paul is telling us peace is a choice, despite what you have done or has been done to you.

First, Paul recognizes that we have these natural worries in life about food and shelter. He encourages us not to shrink from these worries but take them to God in prayer, so he says, "Let your request be made known to God".

As a younger person, I might lay awake for hours staring at the ceiling worrying about the bills, about Liz and Matthew, about the upcoming Session meeting. O, would I worry about the Session meetings! Inevitably, I would go over the same terrain in my mind about all my worries again, and again, and again – getting nowhere. But I would remember, 1 Peter says, "Cast all your anxiety on him because he cares for you."

So I would offer a prayer to God:

> *Please God make the roof stop leaking; keep Liz's heart from breaking; and let there be no querulous, carping, cantankerous, censorious, or complaining people at the Session meeting tomorrow!*

Clearly my prayers needed some work. But they were honest. Surprisingly (not!), they did little to bring peace. My prayers were insufficient because I failed to heed Paul's advice. I left out the thanksgiving. He didn't simply tell us to go to God in prayer, but to do so with thanksgiving.

It puts a frame on our requests. Otherwise prayer might become a long list of complaints. If we shape our prayer requests with thanksgiving, it helps us to realize how much God has already done, giving us confidence and patience with our new requests.

Through taking these worries and shaping them **with thanksgiving**, our mind becomes balanced and centered, so I tried again:

> *Dear God, thank you for my family, my house, and my church...so now, could you please fix it all!?*

Clearly, my prayers still needed work. And it became clear that peace also requires a measure of patience and practice. But I assure you, overtime, as I worked on it, adding the thanksgivings truly did help.

I slept better at night, was more resolute to do my part and, as Paul promised, I felt the peace of God, the sense of holy contentment, a feeling of blessed warmth.

But this is only part one of peace. Ultimately, God and Scripture have higher aims for peace than a good night's sleep. This leads us away from the self-focus of verses 4-7 and into the communal focus of verses 8-9.

In this section, Paul is calling us to turn our mind to noble thoughts. He has moved us away from our own worries into thoughts that take us beyond ourselves. In the first section it was "let *your* requests be made known to God". In this section he calls for our thoughts to be focused on that which is true, honorable, and just.

The deeper peace is not about us as individuals, but about our connections to God and one another.

Peace is such an elusive concept because we have allowed our quest for it to be defined too narrowly. For a greater grasp and a firmer Biblical foundation, we need a clear understanding of just what the word "peace" means.

In Latin, the word is *pax*. This is largely understood as the absence of conflict, as in a truce. During the Roman Empire, the period between 27 BC to AD 180 was marked by a long period without major wars and is known as the *Pax Romana*. But clearly for the Jews and the Christians it was not a time a peace. Jesus was crucified, Christians were fed to lions, and the Jewish temple was destroyed. Biblical peace is a much richer concept than the mere absence of war or a feeling of calm.

In the New Testament, εἰρήνη (*eirene*) is drawn from the verb *eiro* meaning to draw together, to tie together into a whole.

The goal of peace is not simply the absence of conflict, that is two warring parties stepping away, but rather coming together in a new, powerful way. This is what is missing from our quest for a more just and peaceful society – coming together in the name of God. For, by stepping away, we will always be a part – literally, socially, and spiritually.

In this quest, Paul promises us something even more than the peace of God. If we seek this type of reconciliation, he promises the God of peace.

At the end of the first section, when we offer our requests to God, we are given a wonderful peace from God. But, at the end of the second section, it is not a feeling we are left with but rather the very presence of God.

Perhaps the best visual in all the Bible that captures Biblical peace is that of the prodigal son and the running father, uniting in an embrace of reconciliation and love.

Charles Mackesy painted the son as one being held up by the father. He believes the story would be better named as the running father. For the father runs to the son to embrace him, to create Eirene, that is a tying together, in a new powerful way, with the wayward son.

Biblically, peace is not a feeling; it is not the absence of conflict. It is the powerful love of Jesus Christ who ties us together to God the Father with bonds that can never ever, *ever*, *ever*, *ever* be broken.

The most powerful moment of the prodigal son story is that moment of embrace. It does far more to convey the depth of love than words ever could. And at that moment he knew peace, true Biblical peace.

As you look at this painting, you can't make out the face of the son or of the father. But the embrace is clear. The love is clear, and the tying together is unmistakable.

I don't think we should simply consider that embrace as metaphor.

As you consider those you are estranged from, make this embrace your goal. What would need to happen to bring you to this moment with your enemies? – with those you fear? – with those who have wronged you? – or with those you have wronged? Work towards this moment.

Imagine giving that kind of embrace. Imagine receiving it from your Lord. Even as I consider it, a profound peace washes over me. A peace like a river running through my soul.

Amen.

Finding Peace...with the Past...through Forgiveness
Romans 5:1-5

...When you were nine and you let your five-year-old brother's hand go and he ran into the street and was killed... How do you find peace? ...

...When you squandered all your family's money gambling... How do you find peace?...

...When your spouse cheated on you and never pays child support... How do you find peace?...

...When the last time you saw your mother alive and you said horrible things that cannot be unsaid... How do you find peace?...

Traumatic events, that cannot be fixed or undone, can plague us for as long as we live out our days. Too often our strategy is to ignore it, hoping we can forget that it ever happened or pretend that it has no power over us.

But, as Katherine Porter said, "The past is never where you think you left it." What she meant was the past is with you right now; its memories; its impacts.

And, in unexpected moments, the past leaps into the present, at times overwhelming us with grief, regret, and pain. As Southern Gothic novelist Cormac McCarthy observed, "Scars have the strange power to remind us that our past is real." In fact, I have a scar on my hip from a surgery when I was nine years old. Normally, I don't even remember it's there. But, occasionally, I feel a sharp pain and suddenly it all comes back... an extremely sharp pain in my hip and my mother frantically calling an ambulance and six months of recovery.

So, unless we deal properly with the past, we will never truly have peace in the present.

Scripture understands the power of the past to erode our being and our community. In fact, for King David, his past sins ate away at his body. Remember he murdered his lover's husband.

In Psalm 32 he wrote,

> *While I kept silence, my body wasted away*
>
> *through my groaning all day long.*
>
> *For day and night your hand was heavy upon me;*
>
> *my strength was dried up as by the heat of summer.*

Scripture teaches us that peace with the past begins with restoring your relationship with God. Which means repentance that leads to forgiveness.

So, think back to the list at the beginning of this sermon. Consider those parts of your past that still haunt you in the present. Perhaps a part of you has simply accepted that the pain will always be with you.

But if we turn to scripture and trust its words, like Rick Warren we will realize that, "We are products of our past, but we don't have to be prisoners of it."

King David found truth in this, he took the risk and so found peace. He wrote,

Happy are those whose transgressions are forgiven!

In his silence he found grief and pain; in his body, in his mind, in his soul. But when he found the courage to speak, he found happiness and so he wrote,

Then I acknowledged my sin to you,

and I did not hide my iniquity;

I said, 'I will confess my transgressions to the Lord',

and you forgave the guilt of my sin.

As long as we keep quiet about our sins, they will haunt us in ways we cannot imagine. But, as 1 John tells us,

If we say that we have no sin, we deceive ourselves, and the truth is not in us. If we confess our sins, he who is faithful and just will forgive us our sins and cleanse us from all unrighteousness.

Paul knew better than most what it is to need forgiveness. He persecuted and murdered his own people. But he found God's cleansing love and so he found peace; the peace which he described as passing all understanding.

We can't understand it because it does not compute with our accounts. Our natural weak selves keep an accounting of those who have wronged us and what the proportional need for recompense is. And thus, we don't find peace, because some things have no price. But God forgave something we could never repay, which is, in fact, beyond our comprehension.

Paul found peace though he was a wretch: "Therefore, since we are justified by faith, we have peace with God through our Lord Jesus Christ."

This is the foundation of all forgiveness — that of our Lord risen from the grave. The empty cross, which God emptied of wrath, emptied of revenge, emptied of an accounting.

After receiving forgiveness, we then need to go about giving it. Peace with the past is not just about being forgiven, but also about being forgiving.

Pulitzer Prize winner Wallace Stegner wrote, "Be proud of every scar on your heart, each one holds a lifetime's worth of lessons." Those scars reminded us that we have survived and endured.

Perhaps no one used their scars to greater effect then Joseph of the Old Testament. He was his father's favorite. He was a showoff. Life was all about him. But his brothers despised him. Despised him enough to sell him into slavery. It led to years of hardship and horror for Joseph. But years later, he had risen to power and he used it to forgive.

This Way Forward

Remember last week we discovered that Biblical peace is not about the absence of conflict; it is not about stepping away but coming together in a new and powerful way.

It was only through forgiving his brothers that Joseph was able to make peace with his past, which in turn, led to a profoundly beautiful reunion with them.

That was the irenic moment, the moment of peace, of tying him together to his brothers; a moment that perhaps none of them thought would ever be possible again.

If he never forgave them, he would never have his brothers anymore; never have that relationship, that connection; and that would have meant a lifetime of isolation.

Many of us have a hard time forgiving family. There is a moment of disbelief for most when they discover their parents are people too and that they are not perfect.

As you grow into an adult at first their 'peopleness' is a shock. But, if you don't come to peace about it, about how their sins and weaknesses were visited upon you, and shattered your image of your younger days, you will not know peace; you will not know a tying together of all who you are, both the good and the bad.

Which leads us to the last part of forgiveness.

There is one more person to forgive. Once we have received God's forgiveness, and forgiven others sometimes the hardest one to forgive is yourself.

And it is not just forgiveness but acceptance as well. Accepting your own imperfections and your own weakness.

For a long time, the apostle Paul struggled in his weakness. It caused him agony. But in receiving God's forgiveness, he realized that even his weaknesses were meant to draw him to God. Paul heard the Lord say, "My grace is sufficient for you, for **My strength is made perfect in weakness**."

This is a tying together and acceptance of your imperfections and sins – those of your own making and the ones your parents visited upon you – claiming them all while not allowing them to claim you. It is coming to peace with all that you are…the good and the bad.

In this way, our weaknesses become a vehicle to discover the full majesty, power, and glory of God. If Paul never made peace with himself, he never truly could have appreciated the fullness of God's love.

If we can forgive ourselves and others who wronged us, suddenly the past which once haunted us becomes something that shapes us into stronger, more loving, more peaceful people. This is the power of forgiveness; the power of accepting all of who we are.

Remember that Joseph was his father's favorite and something of a brat, flaunting that fancy coat in front of his brothers.

But after years of hardship and heartache, he became something new. When he was able to say to them, "You meant it for evil, but the Lord meant it for good." It was clear he had made peace with their sins. It was also clear that he had moved past his own weaknesses.

It had made Joseph a more loving and humble person because he was at peace with God; he was at peace with his family; and finally, he was a peace with himself. Amen.

Finding Peace...In the Present...Through Contentment
1 Timothy 6:6-8

Yesterday is history, tomorrow is a mystery, today is a gift of God, which is why we call it the present.

I am sure many of you have heard Bill Keane's marvelous quote that reminds us to treasure each moment of life here and now. But sometimes it is a literal present we want most presently!

As a teenager at St. Stephen's Episcopal Day School for Boys I was introduced to the sport of lacrosse. It looked to be a tremendous amount of fun, whipping that ball around while racing up and down the field body checking players out of bounds.

So I begged and pleaded with my mom for months, "I want a lacrosse stick, please let me have a lacrosse stick."

She asked what I was going to do with it: "Are you going to join the lacrosse team?"

"Of course not; that would interfere with golf!"

I just wanted it to mess around with. I was absolutely convinced that I needed this lacrosse stick. I talked about it for months through the fall.

"Mom, I would use it to exercise, for hand-eye coordination, and to help make new friends whenever there is a pick-up lacrosse game. Please!"

Finally, Christmas rolled around and, to my great surprise, there it was! My lacrosse stick! I played with it all Christmas day. It was so much fun! …. And then proceeded to never pick it up again… Last Christmas, my mom reminded me of that fact once again!

But something had gotten a hold of me, making me feel like I absolutely needed this thing in order to be happy, in order to be content! In order to be at peace.

Paul simply tells Timothy, "Be content… with what you have." But is it really that easy? To simply decide that I am at peace with my possessions, my finances, my station in this life? It certainly didn't seem to be once that lacrosse stick was lodged in my brain.

When we are young, we spend a great deal of time and energy grasping for things. For more material goods, more respect in work, and more money in the bank. In Alabama, when the housing boom was at its peak, people were buying these gigantic houses – six thousand square feet! But it was 6,000 nearly empty square feet. They so overspent on the size of their house, that they could not afford to buy furniture. (They could have bought 500 lacrosse sticks for that!)

But something had them convinced that bigger is better – no matter what. At least the neighbors will see what a large house they have or what a nice car they drive. Like that lacrosse stick, this urge, this yearning, this desire, had taken hold of them beyond anything rational.

It certainly didn't seem as easy as simply deciding to be content! If it was, they never would have enslaved their life to that mortgage.

Paul tells Timothy it is a trap and, like a trap, once you've stepped in it, you have been ensnared. And getting out is a whole lot harder than getting in.

For many of those Alabamians, once the market crashed, their problems multiplied. Jobs dried up and now they were deep, deep, deep under water in a house they couldn't afford, with maintenance they couldn't do, spending time wandering through an empty house as a perpetual reminder of their error.

Materialism is a trap that can erode peace… for decades.

But it is not just mania for material things that draw us from contentment; from having peace in the present. It can be anything.

Even those of spiritual profession can fall into the trap of climbing the ladder. Monks aspiring to be the Abbot. Preachers seeking tall steeples.

Centuries ago, Benedictine monks saw the dangers of continually aspiring to be somewhere other than where you were, whether that was a physical place or a place of power or wealth.

Each Benedictine monk must take a vow of stability. A vow that they will spend out their life not only as a monk, but a Benedictine monk. And not only as a Benedictine, but a Benedictine in a particular monastery.

Thomas Merton explains: "By making a vow of stability the monk renounces the vain hope of wandering off to find a 'perfect monastery.' This implies a deep act of faith: the recognition that it does not much matter where we are or whom we live with."

One monastery describes what it means to them,

> *Ultimately there is no escape from oneself, and the idea that things would be better someplace else is usually an illusion.*

This devotion of stability is a strategic decision by the monks. It is an intentional grasping for more God rather than more things. It is their way to live out Isaiah's words:

> *You will keep him in perfect peace, whose mind is stayed on You, because he trusts in You.*

Whenever temptation to look beyond what they have arises, they remember their vow and they turn to God in prayer. Through deep practice, they discover the far-more fulfilling reaches of time with God.

So, in this way, finding peace in the present through contentment is as straightforward as making a choice to be so. But that is when the work begins. The work of prayer and of discipline that over time becomes a part of who you are.

But there is still yet another aspect to being content with our present life – beyond not grasping for more things or grasping more status – and that is not grasping for a return of the past.

This is finding peace with the inexorable march of life.

Sometimes the present marches forward so relentlessly we have a hard time being content with where we are because it keeps changing.

What is it they say about parenthood? "The days are long, but the years fly by."

Many of you know that Wendy and I now have a house filled with emptiness. Oh, it has furniture, but there are no kids.

And, in one sense, there is a newfound peace.

No more fighting over the TV.

No more Wendy telling Matthew to pick up his clothes.

No more teen snark.

(And, to be fair, he will have no more parental hovering either.)

These are the little, lowercase "peaces" in our life; the absence of stressors.

But it is not the kind of peace I want. I am not content with it. Not yet.

Who am I going to watch *Iron Man* with?

This Way Forward

It feels more like a tearing apart; a tearing of our family. But Paul tells us that the key to peace in the present is contentment. Be content with your life. But change is hard. Life is hard.

Finding peace in the present means finding a way to move past the dread of inevitable change that marks life every few years.

Now, I will adjust. And I will come to peace with this change, though it will take some time.

I don't want to be an empty nester, but I know it is right for Liz and Matt to leave the nest; to find their way. I don't like it, so I need to come to peace with it by giving it to God and reminding myself it is best for them.

But if peace is wholeness, then finding peace with change is mending the fabric of your life back together once it's been torn apart – sometimes adding pieces that weren't there before.

I have added something new. I now have something wonderfully new in my relationship with my daughter Liz, who flew the coop ten years ago. We are workout buddies now! We go to the gym twice a week and, on Saturdays, Wendy, Liz, and I go to brunch afterwards!

But there are others tears that are not so easy to mend; other changes that are just as inevitable seem downright cruel: the onset of Alzheimer's, which plagues so many people in our congregation; the relentless disease of Parkinson's; the loss of a spouse or a parent.

These changes don't just create a rip in the fabric of our life, they can tear it to shreds.

If peace is a sense of wholeness and completeness, how can we be content with a present that has torn us into pieces which cannot be sewn back in?

However, even in this, peace is possible. It is a stronger, more powerful peace than simple contentment for our present life.

As things of great value are torn out of our life, it gives us a chance, first of all, to treasure those things that remain. For a loved one with Alzheimer's, singing along with a beloved hymn can mean the world.

But, as pieces are torn out that cannot be replaced, the only thing left to put there is God.

Someone recently shared with me that, in the midst of a debilitating disease, she found that she had only been paying lip service to her faith. As the disease robbed her of the life she once knew, she turned to God and she wove in prayer, she wove in faith, she wove in trust, and she wove in reliance upon God's mercy. She discovered a deeper, a richer, and more powerful faith then she had ever known – one she finds more blessing in, through helping others with similar trials. Truly, it sounds like she has found a measure of peace that could not come without such a harsh trial.

The culmination of Paul's words to Timothy, are found in verses 18 and 19,

> ...*do good, to be rich in good works, generous, and ready to share, thus storing up for [your]selves the treasure of a good*

foundation for the future, so that [you] may take hold of the life that really is life.

Be content with whatever you have, wherever you are, in whatever stage of life you find yourself, so that you, too, may take hold of the life that is really life. Amen.

Finding Peace... in the Future.... through Faith
John 16:31-33

Over the course of this month we have examined the nature of peace. In the first week, we discovered the Biblical foundation for peace focuses not so much on stepping away in the midst of conflict as it does coming together in a new and powerful fashion. In our second week, we explored finding peace with the past through forgiveness. Last week, we discovered that peace in the present comes through contentment and refusing to grasp for more things, for more power, and for a return of the past. This week, we discover that peace with the future comes through faith.

Jesus offers the words in John's Gospel to his disciples during his farewell speech at the Last Supper. This is Jesus' most extended speech and one of the longest in all of Scripture. He knows that, in the future, the disciples are going to face terrific hardships because of their faith in him, but he promises, even in those times, they can have peace in him.

But his words don't stick.

Later after Jesus' death and resurrection, even upon hearing of the good news from Mary Magdalene, they still haven't found peace; they are stuck in fear. They gathered, in fact they huddled together, locking the doors, to keep out the future that faced them. But Jesus passes through a locked door to get to them and declares *shalom, eirene, peace*.

This Way Forward

This is the beginning of a turning point for the disciples. This is when they start to live up to the words, he spoke to them in the 16th chapter of John. He gave them that whole extended speech so that they could have peace.

> *I have said this to you, so that in me you may have peace. In the world you face persecution. But take courage; I have conquered the world!*

By taking a closer look at this verse, we too can find peace in the world – whatever future we face.

Take the word "persecution". Some translations replace it with "tribulation" or "distress". It's hard for us to pin down precisely what Jesus meant, but I think he meant all of these: tribulation in the end times, persecution for the faith, and distress at the dangers the world faces.

These are the various fears we all face in the future and, in all cases, Jesus gives us peace.

There is a lot to fear about the future. In our future, we have the potential for devastating terrorist attacks and environmental collapse due to overpopulation and the abuse of the earth's resources. There is the constant threat of nuclear war, not to mention a random asteroid taking out the planet. And, of course, there is the devastating power of hurricanes – which many discovered all too well last week.

In the face of these endless potential disasters, Jesus tells us his purpose for all his instruction: to grant us peace.

He is not telling us that peace will mean the absence of distress. He said you will have hardship; you will have tribulation; you will have persecution. But he promises, no matter what we face, we can find peace in him.

The secret for this peace is found in his next words, "Take heart".

Once again, the translators have several choices. Others read "take courage" and still more say "be of good cheer". It seems to me each of these different translations is a different opportunity to respond to various futures so that we might have peace.

Take Heart

The distress over our future is our worry, our anxiety over the inevitable outcome of life. There is always loss in our future. It will include the loss of loved ones and the decay of your own body. We fear a life alone and we fear becoming a burden upon our children as we lose our health.

To the distress of the future Jesus says, "Take heart" in other words be comforted by my presence. Remember he declared, "Come to me all you who are weary and carrying heavy burdens… and I will give you rest."

Jesus will be with us and he will be the one to carry the burdens of our heartache and hardship.

So, when you face the distress of impending loss "take heart" and find peace and comfort in Jesus' promise to be by your side.

While some futures require a measure of comfort and acceptance others need bold action.

Good Courage

To this Jesus declares, "Be of good courage."

When our future requires it, there are moments when we will need to stop equivocating, to leap into the fray, to gird our loins. God declares in Deuteronomy,

> *Be strong and courageous. Do not be afraid, for the Lord your God, will never leave you.*

The disciples would need to stand and proclaim Christ in front of dangerous crowds and their lives would run counter to the culture of the time. I am sure they hesitated many times before opening their mouths in his name. But, knowing he would always be right there by their side would give them the strength to act.

This is the near future of our life. It will take work on our part for it to fully become what we hope and intend. We need not be afraid to act, for God will be with us each step of the way. God also promises us in Philippians that we CAN do all things through him who strengthens me.

No matter what we face, if we do it in faith and trust and in a Godly manner, through God we will triumph. *We shall overcome, someday*, was the gospel refrain throughout the civil rights era. The song led to faithful, courageous actions because as the words declared, "The Lord will see us through."

Think about those places in our town and in your life that need you to stand up and speak out. Perhaps there is something illegal and immoral at your place of work. Maybe it is the need to make our town a place where all truly thrive. Perhaps you have felt the Spirit nudging, pushing you, shoving you into action, but fear has held you back and, because of it, you are not at peace. The need to stand up and speak out is haunting you.

Peace through action is what we are trying to do at First Presbyterian. If peace is creating wholeness, a tying together by creating bonds of love, then our work to tie together the races; to tie together the homeless; to tie together the economically poor; to tie together the addicted; to tie together the sinners (that's all of us); to tie together all the people of God, is a peace goal in the Spirit of the call of Christ, "Blessed are the peacemakers."

Peacemaking requires action, but it also requires prayer. To me, the prayer of St Francis is the greatest prayer outside of Scripture – and it is a prayer of action. It begins with "Make me an instrument of your peace." And the action continues. It calls us to sow love, pardon, faith, hope, light, and joy, and to give consolation, understanding, love, and pardon.

Francis did not just pray, it he did it. He lived during The Fifth Crusade and he went to Egypt to meet with a Sultan Malek al-Kamil, in order to find a measure of peace. Next year is the 800th anniversary of this visit. Many of the facts of that visit are lost to the shroud of time. But one thing is clear – he took bold action, risking his life, to pursue God's future.

So, whatever you face in your future, listen to the words of Jesus, "Be of good courage." Act and you will have peace, knowing you have faithfully tried to do the right thing.

As we face the future, we can take heart and take courage, but the final translation is the most intriguing and powerful to my mind.

Be of Good Cheer

"Good cheer" connotes a confidence with positive energy; having absolute certainty of the coming victory of God. In one sense, good cheer almost seems out of place in our world. With all that is happening shouldn't we, at most, have a muted optimism. Being too cheerful might even seem like we don't care about all the suffering, sorrow, and injustice.

Saint Francis faced all the terrors we do, but still exuded this spirit.

The secret of Saint Francis' joyful spirit was his vibrant belief in a God of overflowing goodness and love. Saint Francis was so in love with God that he would pick up two sticks from the ground, tuck one under his chin like a violin, and move the other over it like a bow. Then, in an ecstasy of joy, he would sing, in French, songs of love and praise to God. Francis used to say that he wanted his followers to go about the world like strolling minstrels, "to inspire the hearts of people and stir them to spiritual joy."

(https://www.franciscanmedia.org/author/jack-wintz/)

In addressing the enemy of death, Paul tells the Corinthians, "Behold I tell you a mystery." In other words, "I've got a secret." And when someone is facing a challenge, but is still smiling, you suspect they know something you don't. That is the Christian faith. We have a secret, an open secret, but a special message that gives us ultimate confidence.

We can be of good cheer no matter what, because as we see, in Revelation, God will right every wrong, soothe every heart, restore all broken relationships, and reign as Lord over all things – with such certainty and truth that we will not care that the universe has run out and the stars have been snuffed out, because the "Lord himself will be our light!"

Jesus has overcome the world. His death and resurrection have sealed the promises of our future. His love has conquered death and his grace has set us on the path of eternal life. Our future is absolutely, unequivocally, wholly in the hands of the Lord God of heaven and earth, whose mercy is from everlasting to everlasting. We have peace, knowing the Christ has overcome all things.

500 Years of Reformation: Sola Scriptura
2 Timothy 3:15-17

Five hundred years ago, if you were a European Christian, the church had a strangle hold on your soul. When your husband died, the church might ask for half of your inheritance to get him out of purgatory all that much sooner. In fact, half the wealth of Scotland was in the church. It was assumed the King or Queen were divinely appointed by God, so opposing them meant opposing God and risking eternal damnation. To keep control, the church might execute you if you met in unsanctioned Bible studies or, worse, translated the Bible so people could read it for themselves.

As surely as freeing someone from the basement of a warped kidnapper, so too were the people set free through the Reformation. It might be rightly argued that these reformers unlocked the hearts and minds of people like no other movement in all of history. Without their courage and their devoted scholarship, we would not be here today.

As distant in time as the reformation is, its impact on our world is as clear as if it were yesterday. As a way of coalescing the vast changes made, catch phrases arose both during and after the reformation which are summed up as follows:

> *A sinner is justified by grace alone (sola gratia) through faith alone (sola fide) for the sake of Christ alone (solus Christus), a truth revealed to us in Scripture alone (sola Scriptura).*

For our 500th celebration of the Reformation, we will spend the month of October exploring these Reformation *Solas*, to more fully appreciate its continued influence on our lives.

As the reformation sought to push aside the strangle hold of the church and king, a power vacuum emerged. By whose authority would such sweeping changes be enacted? How would you arbitrate between opposing views? Who would serve as the ultimate authority over people's lives and souls? People would stand or fall not on their fidelity to the church, but their faithfulness to God as interpreted through scripture. Scripture would serve as ultimate arbitrator on matters of faith, especially regarding salvation.

Paul wrote to Timothy to help him remain steadfast in the faith. Paul recites a litany of sins people would be committing. Sins such as: lovers of themselves, lovers of money, boasters, arrogant, ungrateful, slanderers, swollen conceit! Was this written yesterday??!!!

Paul proceeds to tell Timothy that many of these sins are a result of wrong instruction, which prevent people from arriving at the truth and warns him that as the world is being spun in new directions, there is no reason to get caught up in the latest fad.

In contrast, Paul reminds Timothy that ever since he was a child, he has learned the truth from God's sacred writings, especially in regard to salvation through Jesus Christ. Everything we need to know about our reconciliation to God can be found in God's Holy Word.

There is something tremendously comforting about an enduring text, which has not changed for thousands of years. It reminds us that God is the same today, as God was yesterday, and God will be tomorrow. People two thousand years ago in Jerusalem, to those 800 years ago in Turkey, to 200 years ago in China, to today in every corner of the globe have the same truth and, therefore, the same path to our Lord. Everyone is treated the same. That is the perhaps the biggest revolution the Reformation brings to the world.

But a warning about *Sola Scriptura*. Scripture is the ultimate source of truth regarding our salvation in Jesus Christ, but it is not divine in and of itself. The Bible is not the fourth member of the Trinity. We do not worship the Bible, we worship God.

The enduring power of God's Word for over 2000 years does not mean we have a static text. One that was engraved into stone, so to speak.

In contrast to the tablets of stone given to Moses, God chose a different medium for this enduring Word. Rather than author the Bible by the divine hand directly, God chose to fill people with the Holy Spirit, breathing into them divine truth, while allowing their personalities and contexts to come through the writing.

This allows the text to speak to every age, in its own time, through our devoted study to discerning the coherence of the text through the contingent circumstances of the time.

But since it is inspired through people, their culture and personality come through in the text.

Through excessive zeal, people turned the authority of scripture in matters of faith into a sola *scriptura* in all sources of knowledge.

Such abuse led to absurd scientific conclusions like the continued assertion that the earth is the center of the universe. But also dangerous, social ones as well, such as using certain Bible passages to justify slavery and spousal abuse.

With the freedom granted by the reformation comes not only the freedom for good, but greater freedom for sin.

The reformers saw the inherit danger within *Sola Scriptura*. Because, with no other authority to turn to, suddenly each person could justify almost anything based on their individual interpretation! It was not their intent to turn the Bible into an individualistic tool for our personal whims. Instead, they sought to eliminate those traditions that had no basis in scripture while, as one scholar noted, "retaining the strength found in a traditional way of reading Scripture within a community of faith."

This approach is rooted in scripture itself, particularly in Paul's letter to Timothy.

Before declaring all scripture is inspired and useful for teaching, Paul tells Timothy, "Now you have observed my teaching, my conduct, my aim in life, my faith, my patience, my love, my steadfastness, my persecutions, and my suffering," and then goes on to say, "continue in what you have learned and firmly believed, knowing from whom you learned it."

This means scripture does not come to us in a vacuum and, normally, should be interpreted in light of faithful Christians who have come before us.

Thus, Timothy's and our understanding of God's holy Word is shaped by faithful people who both share with us the meaning of the text and show us how to live it out.

There are texts that have spoken to me directly. No doubt. But the ones that speak most powerfully to me are those that have been passed down by my teachers, my family, and you. They have opened Bible texts to me in ways I never would have discovered on my own.

The scrolls of your favorite Bible verses are filled with quotes from Philippians. At first, I wondered why. I love that letter, but why so many? It turns out many of you are in a class on Philippians. And those teachers have opened that letter to you, multiplying your appreciation for it.

It is this that makes scripture come alive, in ways that often our individual study cannot match.

Before seminary, for me, Deuteronomy was just a book written a long time ago. Though it was God's Word, it only had tangential relation to my life of faith. Then I took a course from Patrick Miller. As Professor Miller disclosed the context behind its chapters and its role in the life of the Jews, suddenly Deuteronomy sang. The verses which had previously struck me as needlessly repetitious, suddenly harmonized and resonated the Jews struggles and joy with their relation to Yahweh, the law, and the Promised Land.

The Holy Spirit used Professor Miller to sanctify it verses in my soul.

Ever since a child I have been drawn to the 23rd Psalm.

As I have said it with you through scores of funerals, its power to speak through death has grown. As we have sung it together in worship, the beauty of God's presence has multiplied. As you have shared with me, its power to see you through cancer, lost jobs, and failed relationships, the notion of the Shepherd God has sunk much deeper into my soul. I could literally go on for hours with various other scriptures.

The reformers, through prayer and study, taught us that we need go no further than scripture to find God's promise and path for salvation. When you have lost your moorings turn to the Word. The Holy Spirit continues to connect us to its power and wonder through the voice, words, and hearts of each other. Amen.

500 Years of Reformation: Sola Fide
Romans 3:21-22

During the period leading up the Reformation, the process of forgiveness could best be described as an accounting system. The debts you accrued through your sins could be paid in various ways. Going to the confessional and being assigned certain tasks by your priest might include saying various prayers so many times, along with a promise to do your best. But literal payment was also included. One could build a church or endow a Mass on behalf of the dead, to pay for a loved one's sins, thus springing them out of purgatory. Think about this for a moment. Think about someone you have lost. Now picture them trapped in purgatory fulfilling the punishment for sins not yet purified. You would pay most any amount to free them. The church knew this and used it to great financial advantage.

This accounting system of forgiveness became so crass and flagrant there was even a jingle used by the Pope's emissary to raise funds for St Peter's, "Every coin in the coffer rings a soul from purgatory springs." If Jesus had been around at the time, turning over money changers' tables would have been the mildest of his reactions.

Furthermore, it not only cost coin but it tortured souls to keep up with their sins. All sins committed post-baptism needed to be confessed. If one died with unconfessed sins it could mean more time in purgatory or, perhaps worse, eternal damnation. Such beliefs account for Martin Luther's famous marathon confessions. After one especially picayune session, Luther's confessor told him not to come back until he had committed some really "good" sins.

This system of accounting was exacerbated by the belief that the church was *appointed as God's official voice on earth*. This meant paying homage, not so much to God but to God's supposed emissary. As you can imagine, with the church engaging in wars, torturing heretics, and robbing widows of money, it was especially hard to tolerate for your everyday disciple.

Clearly, dramatic reform was needed and *Sola Fide*, which means "by faith alone", summed it up nicely.

No earthly regent held God's salvific power, nor could any good work or ritual observance earn you a place in heaven.

This problem of works righteousness was not new to the Reformation, however. In fact, religious leaders, claiming to be the authority on people's souls, have always been a problem.

In the time of the Old Testament, it centered on ritual purity. Through avoiding certain foods and people, along with proper observance of ritual animal sacrifice, it was thought one could reconnect to God. Though clearly prescribed in God's law, these rites were never meant to be substitutes for trust and love.

In the time of the prophets, God made his thoughts clear, in no uncertain terms, about the corruption of these rituals. In Amos, God declared

I hate, I despise your festivals,

...Even though you offer me your burnt-offerings and grain-offerings,

I will not accept them....

But let justice roll down like waters, and righteousness like an ever-flowing stream.

Even though the people were following the ritual observances, they failed in their love of neighbor and love of God. As in Amos' time it was with Paul and so he writes,

But now, irrespective of law, the righteousness of God has been disclosed, and is attested by the law and the prophets, the righteousness of God through faith in Jesus Christ for all who believe.

It is solely by God's grace that we are saved, and we receive this grace through trust in our Lord, *sola fide,* by faith alone. It was not through endless confessions or baptism. It is not through animal sacrifice or ritual observance. It does not come through an intermediary, but directly from God's heart to your soul.

There is no age that does not distort the path to salvation. In the time following the Reformation, up until today, people have twisted the nature of faith.

Biblically, the faith called for is multi-dimensional. In part, it is an intellectual agreement that indeed Christ is Lord. Scores of evangelistic crusades raced to get people to say, *I believe Jesus is the Son of God*, as if that phrase, in and of itself, had magical power to extricate one from damnation and open the gates of heaven. Almost like believing *"Open Sesame"* can make a locked door dramatically open. It does not work! Believe me, I tried many times as a child!

The deeper concept of faith, the Bible calls us to again and again, is trust. The essence of faith is trust. Faith is not about *believing* all the right things.

It is this entirely, erroneous assumption that has so dramatically and disastrously divided God's house. We have so fooled ourselves, that we believe our opinions about God are more significant than our trust in God. This is a subtle, but fundamentally important, distinction.

Imagine you need lifesaving surgery. You find a surgeon who has a perfect record of saving her patients, 100%! You read an article which delineates the reason for her success and attributes it to her nerves of steel and keen, analytical mind. You're sold! Then you read another article. It claims her willingness to buck conventional procedures in the heat of the moment, in order to find creative solutions in the blink of an eye, makes all the difference.

Suddenly, the Twittersphere is exploding with heated debates. People are calling each other names because of their opinions on this surgeon. You believe the analytical group is right. It is her keen mind that makes all the difference.

In the end, despite all the heated debate and despite your own opinion, none of this matters. Your life does not depend upon your opinions concerning this surgeon's gifts nor the opinions of others; your life depends upon your willingness to go under the knife. It depends on your trust in her. She is the one who will do the saving.

Sadly, since the beginning, Christians have been divided, sometimes deeply and sometimes to the point of murder, over differences on how Christ saves. Some of these differences are important, but none more important than this simple truth. Jesus saves us; not our correct beliefs. All we are called to is trust, even though none of us fully understand.

The Lutheran Catechism says it this way, "I believe that I cannot by my own reason or strength believe in Jesus Christ, my Lord."

Once we understand that the essence of faith is trust, we can also clear up the debate between faith and works.

Our instincts tell us that good people go to heaven and bad people don't. This is because of our inherent sense of fairness. But Jesus turned fairness on its head and Scripture tells us that no one is righteous, not even one. There are no people who are "good enough" to get to heaven on their own.

For Luther, the role of faith in salvation was so central that he even wanted to take James' epistle out of the Bible. Phrases like "faith without works is dead" gave him pause.

But works have always been central to Scripture's call for believers. Paul's point in Romans is that we must not fool ourselves into believing that our good works will cause our salvation. Instead, those works are an outgrowth of it.

Sola fide, that is we are saved through faith alone, was not meant to eradicate the tension between faith and works. Rather, it was to underscore the necessity of faith, on the one hand, and the impossibility of our works earning us a ticket to heaven, on the other.

And yet, since faith is ultimately trust in God rather than simple belief in God, works will inevitably follow. Trust, by definition, demands action and risk taking, based on belief. If you don't act on your trust, then it is not really trust. Galatians teaches us that a true, living faith works by love.

A living faith works by love. I've known this concept my whole life. But it has never hit me between the eyes until recently. This past week I met someone who embodies this love, courage, and risk for his faith, perhaps better than anyone alive today.

India is plagued by slavery – over 18 million. One man, Pastor Praveen Chakravarty, daily risks his life to rescue child slaves sold into open-pit mines to live their short lives in brutal conditions. During the day they work in the devilishly, hot sun and at night they endure the cruelest of abuse at the hands of their captors. The worst stuff of nightmares you can imagine. I told you a portion of this story about Pastor Chakravarty some months ago but, when I met the man, it multiplied my sense of awe at his love and courage. He told us about how his family became Christian.

His grandfather was a snake charmer – literally. He made his money entertaining crowds on the street. One day, he fell in the river and was drowning. He called on his gods, but none came to help. He decided to reach out to Jesus: "If you save me Jesus, I will follow you." Someone thrusts their hand in the river and snatched him out and he devoted the rest of his life to the gospel ministry.

Praveen follows in his footsteps, spreading the gospel, and he has built a network of thousands of pastors all who risk their lives to spread the love of Christ.

Without any sense of drama, self-pity, or fear he described how he became enemy number one of the quarry miners. By freeing their labor force and finally getting the government to enforce the laws, he cut into their profits.

He wasn't worried; that was until they began to threaten his mother as well. Once they realized fear and threats would not shake him, they began threatening her. His mother is fine but don't let that fool you. These are not idle threats. Last year over 160 pastors in his network were murdered, martyred for their faith.

But he does not hesitate. For his purpose is born out of love. Love for Jesus Christ who redeemed and saved him. Love for these forgotten children, thousands of whom now have someone who loves them back. Even during his brief week in America, 700 more children were rescued through his organization.

We access God's grace through faith in our Lord Jesus Christ. It is easy to believe. But deep faith requires risk, which means courage and action. Let's not only put our faith in Jesus to rescue our souls, let's trust that his way is the right way and act in bold love in his name for the most vulnerable in our world. Amen.

500 Years of Reformation: Sola Gratia
Romans 3:23-24

Since all have sinned and fall short of the glory of God; they are now justified by his grace as a gift, through the redemption that is in Christ Jesus,

You're going to get a mansion; you're going to get a mansion. Everybody here is going to get a mansion! In fact, if you tell others to come, they will too!

That is grace. That heavenly mansion God offers us all.

This week's Latin catch phrase, *Sola Gratia*, arose out of the Reformers concern that during their age the church was placing too much emphasis on the believer's participation in the process of their salvation. That somehow, in order for God's salvific grace to be effective, the believer had to respond with good works, to cooperate. Salvation depended upon God *and us*.

But for Calvin, such a notion was anathema!

Through his examination of scripture, he saw a pattern. Salvation depended entirely upon God. This was the point of the Salvation history in the Old Testament. Time and again, God chose those with deeply imperfect faiths to be key cogs in the divine plan to reconcile humanity. Those choices underscored that salvation comes not because of our heroic faith and intrinsic worth, but solely out of God's deep love and his tireless effort to draw us to Him.

It is true that it is through faith alone, that is trust, that we receive this gift of salvation, but it is solely because of God's grace that this gift is even offered to us at all. If faith/trust is the how of salvation, then grace is the why. Just because God loves us.

As Paul declares in Romans, we are justified by grace as a gift.

To unpack this rather dense theology I propose, first of all, that you think of this grace as a literal gift. As it has been said, mercy is not getting what you deserve (i.e. punished), but grace *is getting* what you do not deserve (i.e. salvation). Imagine this gift is that pearl of great price Jesus refers to, with a bright red bow wrapped around it.

We are given this gift

despite our unworthiness,

> beyond what we could possibly be worth,

>> never taken away when we prove unworthy,

>>> and we fully enjoy its worth when we receive it in faith…

Despite our unworthiness.

Despite our unworthiness, everyone who has ever lived has this supremely radiant pearl with their name on it. Even though everyone of us has unequivocally shown that we won't take proper care of it, that we will take it for granted, and furthermore will use it more for our own benefit than that of others, God still gives it to us. This unworthiness is our sin.

Paul tells us in Romans, "All have sinned and fallen short of the glory of God." The favorite hymn of so many people sums up the perfect response to this grace,

> *Amazing grace! How sweet the sound that saved a wretch like me!*

It is a sweet sound indeed! Of course, we know that this hymn's author was a slave trader who saw the light of God's love and had a change of heart. But that is not what Paul is talking about here. No. Grace is not about an especially unique sinner, but every single one of us! From a human perspective, we feel as if there is some dramatic distinction between sinners.

But from God's perspective,

>All Fall Short...

>All of us.

But not only is this gift given despite our unworthiness, it is given beyond what we could possibly be worth. This is the next layer of God's grace.

Even if we had lived a perfect life, this glorious pearl is worth far more than we could have ever earned, even with a perfect track record!

It would be like giving me a Stradivarius violin, instead of someone who had devoted their life to this art, practicing painstakingly for decades while, at the same time, studying the history behind the instrument and its maker. All those years of blood and sweat makes that person the logical choice. I simply don't have the intrinsic talent to ever be able to fully appreciate such a gift.

Salvation is not given to us because God sees potential in us – as if we were gold, tarnished by sin, that just needs some buffing out to restore our intrinsic worth.

Even if we were perfect, there is nothing that would compel God to offer us an eternal blessing of being part of the family of heaven. Think about the flowers of the field. They neither toil nor spin, nor sin; yet they are only here for a time and then gone. But, through God's free gracious love, it is given to us all, not simply those with the most inherent potential.

In fact, in order to demonstrate the primacy of grace, God takes special care in the history of salvation, not to simply recruit those with the most potential the way we might assemble, perhaps a football team or a dance troupe.

Catholic scholar Bishop Barron wrote,

> Absolutely essential to the biblical witness and to the best of the Christian spiritual tradition is the assertion that the divine love comes first …The Lord didn't ask Simon's permission or assess whether he was the most effective fisherman; he just got into the man's boat and commenced to

give orders. And Jesus sums up this principle of the primacy of grace with admirable directness: "You did not choose me, but I chose you" (John 15:16)

But God's grace goes to even greater lengths. Not only does it come despite our unworthiness and beyond what we could possibly be worth, it is never taken away no matter how unworthy we prove to be.

This doctrine is known as the perseverance of the saints, or "once saved always saved." Even though God gives us this beautiful, gorgeous pearl when we did not deserve it and then we trashed it at a late-night bender, God does not take it back.

God, the gracious giver, is also the steadfast lover, no matter how poorly we treat this grace.

One place to see this scriptural warrant is in the eleventh chapter of Romans, "The gifts and call of God are irrevocable."

Again and again, we see throughout the Old Testament, God remains faithful to Israel even when they stray. They are the chosen people; chosen utterly by God's grace and time and again they spurn that gift through worshipping idols abusing the poor and violating God's laws.

Jesus comes back to his disciples – even after they fled in fear to protect themselves by abandoning him at the cross.

This is unconditional grace. Salvation begins and ends with God. Period.

It would have been enough if God had given grace despite our unworthiness,

> it would have been enough had God given it beyond what we could possibly be worth.

> > It would have been enough had God never taken it away when we prove unworthy,

> > > but God gives it to us when we don't even think this gift is worth being had.

God is not simply casting a net hoping to catch some people for the heavenly places, rather as Paul tells us, "they are justified!" All have sinned and *they* are now justified by his grace as a gift.

All have this eternal love of God.

For those who have followed Calvin's thinking, this is known as irresistible grace. God, who is Lord of the universe cannot ultimately be thwarted by mere human striving.

In Acts 13:48 "When the Gentiles heard this, they were glad and praised the word of the Lord; **and as many as had been destined for eternal life became believers**."

It turns out that even our faith we have in Jesus is a gracious, free gift from the Lord. Everything to do with our salvation belongs to God. That is grace, it comes freely, irresistibly, and will never be withdrawn. Thanks be to God!

500 Years of Reformation: Solus Christus
Acts 4:12

In the midst of our month-long celebration of the 500th anniversary of the Reformation, on this Kirkin' Sunday we would do well to turn to John Knox. He grew up in an age when the church of Scotland owned more than half the real estate and "gathered an annual income 18 times that of the crown."* Many of the bishops lived immoral lives and priests were political appointees, who often did nothing more than collect an income. In fact, the archbishop of St Andrews sired 10 children through multiple concubines.[1]

Against this corruption and violence of the church, ever the fiery preacher, Knox encouraged the people to rebel, telling them it was their duty. And he boldly stood by them with such vigor that one man standing before his grave said, "Here lies a man who neither flattered nor feared any flesh."

Knox had such courage because he knew his eternal fate was not in the hands of the church, but solely and squarely in the hands of Christ. *Solus Christus* teaches us that Christ is the sole mediator between us and God; there is no middleman on earth we have to go through.

---

[1] (http://www.christianitytoday.com/history/people/denominationalfounders/john-knox.html)

The Biblical warrant for this is found in Hebrews, "You are a royal priesthood." Every believer can lay claim to this because as Acts teaches us, the "Spirit has been poured out on all flesh." This doctrine demonstrates that in the worldwide family of the church, there is no preferred denomination. All have equal access which comes through Christ.

However, *Solus Christus*, by Christ Alone, is not only about access to God. To see how Christ is the key behind all things, we turn to Acts and the time of the early church.

After the resurrection, when Peter had received forgiveness from Christ for abandoning him, suddenly Peter turns the corner. He goes from being shifting sand to the solid rock upon which Christ founds his church. In the course of a few days, he healed a man and converted scores to Christ, which led to a profound sharing, so powerful, that Acts tells us that all who believed were of one heart, that everything was held in common…and there was not a needy person among them! This all happened solely through the power of Christ.

In our passage this morning, he speaks with bold courage to the authorities who had taken Jesus' life and could just as well take his. The chief priests had Peter taken prisoner and brought him and John before the high council and demanded to know by what authority and power they did this healing. "Let it be known to all of you, and to all the people of Israel, that this man is standing before you in good health by the name of Jesus Christ of Nazareth."

In other words, it was done "By Christ alone."

Fearing that this would spread, they threatened Peter and John in attempt to silence them. Without flinching, Peter declares, "Whether it is right in God's sight to listen to you rather than to God, you must judge; for we cannot keep from speaking about what we have seen and heard."

In other words, we must answer to Christ Alone.

Peter is underscoring that it is by God's authority that we speak not chosen representatives here on earth. Martin Luther took a similar stand when he was called before Emperor Charles V to recant his beliefs. Whether he uttered the following famous words or not is up for debate but certainly they contain the essence of his message. It was reported that after spending considerable time defending his works point-by-point he concluded by saying, "Here I stand; I can do no other. God help me."

It is the position of Martin Luther that grew into our current understanding that our moral selves do not stand, or fall based on the earthly authorities we answer to, but to Christ alone.

Peter's bold stance was built upon a deep grasp of the nature of faith in Christ. But their actions before the Council were not a result of pre-planned political actions; they came because of an act of love.

Before they were arrested, Peter and John were going to the temple to pray. As they were passing through the gate, a man lame from birth asked them for alms. Now, it is likely most every one of us have had a similar encounter. Think about your last time. Think about how anxious you were. Think about all the excuses your recited in your head. As you were passing by that man or woman, were your thoughts about them and their needs or about you and your anxiety?

Peter and John were not people of means. He turned to the man and says look at us! As if to say, your begging from us. See how we are dressed; we are hardly in a position to offer you alms. And then he proceeds to say, what are for me, some of the most powerful words in all of scripture. Whenever I recite them, I feel a power flow through me that resonates beyond the simple words. "Silver and gold have I none, but in the name of Jesus Christ stand up and walk!"

When I hear these words, I think I can feel what that man felt on that day. But it is beyond imagining what he felt when, for the first time in his life, he stood on his own two feet.

Peter had no gold; he had no silver. He had *Solus Christus*, Christ alone and it was more than enough to give the man more than he dared to hope for.

There are so many things we want in this world. Food. Shelter. Financial security. Health Care. Safe homes. These are important, but Peter knew something. He knew we may want one thing in life, but Christ alone gives us more than we could ever receive in all the silver and gold in the world.

He gives us himself.

After seeing that man stand, wait, not just stand but he saw him, walk, and leap and praise God. (Picture it! Can you see it?) After seeing this, after feeling the power of God flow through his heart and soul, Peter would have been able to stand up before those in power and, without flinching, claim that, with Christ, he has no fear.

The things of this world are as nothing and the powers of this world are like flies compared to the power and love of God in Jesus Christ.

In Peter's words, I feel the certainty of the absolute destined power of Jesus to heal ALL ills; to redeem ALL creation, to reconcile ALL humanity; to tear the curtain that divides God and humanity. In Christ alone we come as one; and before Christ together we kneel in homage to our Savior, our Master, our Friend, our Comforter, and our Lord.

Whenever you feel fear, whatever trepidation strikes you this coming week; when you are so low and you can't go any lower; when you face the worries of this world and they have knocked you off your feet, when you are feeling lame in your heart, lame in your soul . . . hear those words of Peter as if they are spoken to you, "Silver and gold have I none but in the name of Jesus Christ, stand up and walk!" Stand up and praise God! Leap for the Lord with the joy who comes to know that Christ alone gives you all that you need!

Jesus is our all in all through which our life and all life came into being and the destiny for which we are headed. The Bible begins with Jesus, when God said, "Let there be light." Jesus was that word. The Bible ends with Jesus, when in Revelation scripture's very last words declare, "The grace of the Lord Jesus be with all the saints. Amen." And Amen.

Awkward Verses... An Eye for An Eye
Matthew 5:38-42; Exodus 21:22-24

Presbyterians are people of the Book, that is, all we believe and do is based upon the Bible. But, clearly, there are passages we no longer follow and some things we believe even seem contrary to Scripture.

This month, we will be exploring those texts which prove problematic or inconvenient for our beliefs today. We will look at verses in the New Testament which, at first glance, seem to deny women's leadership roles. We will examine how we hold true to Scripture while fully affirming the call of women to ordained ministry in the church. We will discover that historic interpretations of verses used to restrict the role of women in the church do not hold up under closer scrutiny.

At the end of the month, we will turn to Ananias and Sapphira, members of the fledgling Christian community in Acts. We believe that God is one of grace and forgiveness, seen most clearly in Jesus Christ. But, when Ananias and Sapphira failed to pledge their resources to God, they were struck dead! That hardly seems merciful and gracious.

Today, we will dive deeper into the Exodus passage that calls for an "eye for an eye and a tooth for a tooth"! It is in the Bible, so we are supposed to follow it – right? Old Testament justice, it is called. Sometimes, it is referred to as "the law of retaliation". There was even a movie entitled "Eye for an Eye" with Sally Fields, who exacts revenge upon the murderer of her children. It is inconvenient for our faith today because we believe God calls us to the opposite of revenge – to forgiveness. Jesus teaches us to forgive those who have wronged us.

How do we account for this change?

The Old Testament law is clear. It does not equivocate – an eye for an eye. Yet, Jesus offers something radically new.

Did God used to be a really angry God and, when he had a son, he became soft on crime? What changed? How did we go from an eye for an eye to turn the other cheek? I suppose Jesus would never be elected as a district attorney; nor a bench judge – no death penalty; no harsh sentences.

But rather than dismissing this passage as outdated, through a closer look at the context, we will discover how this Exodus passage still has power to speak to us today, while finding that Jesus' reinterpretation moves us into a higher calling.

Remember, in Biblical times as people settled into cities from nomadic living, a complex social hierarchy took hold in the ancient world. Those in authority were exalted, as in the case of the Egyptian pharaoh – all the way to the status of godhood.

This was not simple, social stratification. It was an embedded belief that those of higher social status were qualitatively superior to those beneath them. Because of this, justice was meted out with a clear bias toward those with greater power and wealth.

In other words, if a slave broke his master's arm, he would be killed for it. That was what justice would have dictated.

Now consider the Hebrew people. They spent hundreds of years in the clutches of the pharaoh with all its cultural baggage. As God delivered them into the Promised Land, the Lord sought a different way of living for them and a profoundly different understanding.

All people are created in God's image. Every single one. That is what Genesis teaches us. This means, first of all, that no person is inherently of greater value because of their social station. Secondly, each life is precious to God.

Now I don't mean to imply that Israel was a land of equality and equal opportunity – it wasn't. They carried much of the social problems and prejudices that they learned in Egypt for centuries, as did most all cultures of that time. For one, slavery was simply accepted, and the role of women was still one of a second or third-class citizen.

And yet, this law of God, in Exodus, an eye for an eye and a tooth for a tooth was not a law of revenge or Wild West justice. It was, in fact, the opposite.

It was a statement that no life is of more value than the other. So, if the slave takes out his master's eye, then his punishment is to have his eye taken, not his life. Or if someone steals a loaf of bread, you don't cut off his arm.

Practically, this meant a monetary amount was required that was considered the equivalent value of the loss incurred. Except in the case of murder. if a person in power takes the life of another, then his life shall be taken. No special breaks for the wealthy.

Instead of a law of revenge, this passage discloses a growing awareness that the nature of this God was one of love for all people.

Remember that in the Promised Land the law of the land and the religious instruction were the same. There was no such thing as the separation of church and state in those days.

So, these statutes in Exodus served as the laws of governance for the people of Israel. These were the laws that held the community together.

An eye for eye was a lesson in equal justice, establishing laws that mitigated against wanton revenge. Its purpose was to forge the people of Israel into a nation built on God's laws.

But then Jesus comes along and offers something new, saying,

> *You have heard that it was said, "An eye for an eye and a tooth for a tooth." But I say to you, do not resist an evildoer.*

"You have heard that it was said...." Right away, Jesus' choice of words challenges the Old Testament. Rather than treating them as a law of God from Scripture, he seems to be treating them as a saying. "You have heard" demonstrates Jesus' belief that this law no longer serves its original purpose.

Jesus is the one who sets the example for setting aside Biblical laws when they no longer serve God's will. You and I now understand how that law helped create a more-just society in its time and place. No more privilege. But in our time, and apparently in Jesus' time, an eye for an eye evoked notion of bloody revenge.

Jesus has another, deeper, greater purpose than equal punishment. The key is found in his rationale for calling us to turn the other cheek.

But I say to you, do not resist an evildoer.

The law of an eye for an eye was for fair justice for the victim. Jesus call of non-resistance is out of love for the one whose heart is filled with evil.

Jesus is not trying to establish a new law of the land, but a principle by which his followers can change the world through changing what lies within us.

Jesus believes that people's hearts will be transformed when we refuse to return evil for evil.

Jesus demonstrated the truth and power of this strategy when he turned the other cheek while being lifted up onto the cross. He prayed not for justice, as he hung there, but for forgiveness for his killers. He sought to transform their hearts from hate to love. And on that day, as Jesus drew his last breadth, that is exactly what happened to a Roman guard who, seeing the way in which he died, declared, "Truly this man was God's son!"

His heart changed, forever.

In this world we fight hard for justice and we should. We need to live in a land where all are treated equally. Thousands of years ago an "eye for an eye" was the beginning of that path.

It was a growing awareness that all people are of equal value in God's eyes.

But a land of equal justice is only the beginning. The law will never save humanity. It won't save our country. It won't bring harmony or peace, because the hearts of men will always find a way to denigrate, steal from and destroy their neighbor, no matter the laws you put down on the books.

India has more slaves than any other country in the world. They are taught that God made them this way. That God is punishing them for sins in another life. And that they are literally worth nothing.

First Presbyterian Church is working with Set Free Alliance to free these children. They have rescued over 22,000. They have set them free and brought them justice.

But they have given them so much more than physical freedom. There is a video in which the children are holding signs, "I was hate" "I was a slave" "I was mad at God" ... but now I am free ... now I love to play ... now I have friends ... now I am in love ... now I am excited ... now I love Jesus.

They have been taught that God loves them. That they are precious. That they are made in his image. And now they're not only free in body, but they are free in mind.

God calls us to be stewards – of our time and our money – we are to pledge them to God (but not turned into the church office!).

Yes, to bring justice. Yes, to bring peace. But more than anything, to bring the good news of the Gospel! These children have received it. Many of these children now have jobs and they have given back over $300,000 to help save other children – to share the love of God.

Let our generosity, our passion, and our love be equal to that of these children.

They have discovered the love of God and there is no revenge in their hearts.

Do not resist an evil doer; and you, too, can change the world one heart at a time.

Awkward Verses... Women Should Have Authority Over Their Head
1 Corinthians 11

As we continue exploring those Biblical verses that prove problematic for our faith today, let's return to a text whose topic is still a matter of debate within the Christian world – the role of women in the church.

This verse is problematic for us today because, at first glance, it makes it seem like we are out of step with the Bible. After all, we have women leaders in our church; women who have authority over men.

In our community of Spartanburg there are dozens of churches that will not ordain a woman to pastoral ministry and would claim we have abandoned clear Biblical teaching.

But I am convinced, without a shadow of a doubt, that we are fully in-line with Jesus' will for our church. We can clearly see the tremendous gifts women bring to ministry. Jesus said, "you will know them by their fruits". And the fruits of their ministry are unequivocal.

In my life, I have only known a denomination which ordains women. You don't grow up with Abigail Evans as your mother and have any doubts that the Lord God has called her to proclaim the Good News. But many people did, at least when they first met her.

At Broadway Presbyterian in New York, her office was by the front door, so most people assumed she was the receptionist. A typical exchange went as follows,

> "I would like to see a pastor."

> "I am a pastor."

> "Oh, I don't want to see you. I don't believe in women minsters."

> "Well, you'll have to talk to God because God called me to be a pastor – God put me here."

Her reception in Pikeville was no better. In the mountains of Kentucky, they didn't have enough pastors, so the Presbytery often sent pastors to the churches. She served as an evangelist/pastor to 3 churches in the Appalachian hollows.

When she arrived to preach one Sunday someone asked her,

> "What are you doing here?"

> "I'm your preacher."

> "Oh, I guess there wasn't anyone else."

In time, they came to embrace her for her courage to navigate narrow mountain roads to be there every Sunday.

When she was called to the ministry, all the ordination certificates still had "He's" printed all over them, so they simply crossed out the "He's" and hand wrote in "She's"!

It was the culture of the time, but it was also the history of Biblical interpretation. Over the centuries the translations themselves grew more biased against women ministers than the Greek texts themselves did.

As we look at our verse, *women should have authority over their head* we will find that this verse presents a challenge for the modern reader. Not because it contradicts our beliefs, as some would claim, but because of the challenge of translation.

The Bible was written in a time and culture entirely different language than our own. This makes translations notoriously difficult and requires a series of choices by the translator which, often, discloses their own cultural bias rather than that of the Bible.

In fact, we shall see the main culprit is not the culture from Paul's time nor our being out of step with Scripture. The main problem is the misreading of this passage to perpetuate the hegemony of male-dominated leadership, that is not supported by a thorough, unbiased reading of the text.

Whereas the Bible can be grasped in a second – God is love – it also needs to be wrestled with for a lifetime.

By the end of this sermon, you will see it means the exact opposite of what people assumed for centuries!!

The history of interpretation is perhaps best summed up in *Matthew Henry's Bible Commentary*,

> "The woman was made subject to man... made for his help and comfort. And she should do nothing, in

Christian assemblies, which looked like a claim of being equal."

Matthew Henry and others believed this passage was telling women that men should be in authority over her. And, let's face it, that she should essentially be his maidservant. But this interpretation does not hold up under closer scrutiny.

The Greek word used here for authority is *exousian* and that expresses our own power that we have from God. For example, it is used to describe Jesus' power to expel demons and his authoritative preaching.

The word is not used as one exercising authority over another. If that were the case, the word would be *exousiantes*. Secondly, prepositions are notoriously difficult to translate from one language to another. The key preposition in our verse is *epi*. And that word is translated, just to name a few: by, in, on, upon, at, to, unto, and over.

So, the King James translates the verse as, "ought the woman to have power on her head" – meaning a man ruling over her, but the NIV reads, "a woman ought to have authority over her own head" – meaning she speaks without a man's authority over her when she prophesies.

This explains the convoluted argument concerning covering her hair.

In Paul's culture, a woman's hair was a sign of her womanhood and, therefore, of her husband's authority over her. In these verses, Paul is telling us that when prophesying, a woman should cover her head so that she is symbolically no longer under the man's authority. The gift comes directly from God.

Historically, this passage was interpreted to say: that a man should be in authority over the woman; but it seems that Paul, at least with regards to prayer and prophecy, was saying the exact opposite! That a woman should have authority over "HER OWN HEAD".

It is true, in general, that in that culture a woman was under her husband's authority. But Paul was offering a new teaching. When it came to a woman proclaiming God's truth, she did it on her own because the word came directly from God.

Some who persist in denying women's leadership in churches might capitulate on this verse but would claim that 1 Timothy 2:12 unequivocally bars women. The New Living Translation reads, "I do not let women teach men or have authority over them. Let them listen quietly." This translation makes it sound like Paul is creating a generalization. But in the Greek the word is "woman" – singular. The purpose of this letter was to squelch false doctrine that was being taught in Ephesus:

> *As I urged you when I went into Macedonia, stay there in Ephesus so that you may command certain people not to teach false doctrines any longer ... they do not know what they are talking about...* (1 Timothy 1:3-4, 7)

Furthermore, the word translated here as "authority" only occurs once in all the Bible, *authentein*, and a more accurate translation for this word would be "domineer" as it is in the

Latin Vulgate, or "usurp authority" as in the New English Bible. Thus, a better translation might read as follows:

I do not permit a woman to domineer a man.

Since Paul was correcting specific, false teachers and this passage is in the singular, Paul was speaking about a specific woman not creating a universal principle.

The next argument offered against female preachers claims that there were no female apostles. But that is not true either. At the end of Romans, Paul writes of an Apostle named Junia. In early Christians centuries it was assumed to be a woman, since that name is feminine and never refers to a male.

But in later translations, scribes added an "S" making it a male name. In the 1800's the name was purposefully changed to Julian. A clear choice by translators to perpetuate preconceived notions rather than interpreting the text with the best scholarship possible.

So, even though the New Testament was socially conditioned by the cultural roles of men and women in its time, it also clearly began to see, as Paul writes in Galatians, "there is no longer slave nor free, male nor female, Jew nor Greek."

Lastly, we must ask ourselves: What is the root of woman's submissive role in society? Perhaps you've wondered why it has been this way for so many thousands of years.

You've read it before, but perhaps it never sunk in. In the first chapter of Genesis we are told, "In the image of God, he created them male and female he created them." At that point there is no qualitative distinction made between the two sexes.

It is not until after The Fall in chapter 3 that we read,

> *To the woman he said, "I will greatly increase your pangs in childbearing; in pain you shall bring forth children, yet your desire shall be for your husband, and he shall rule over you."*

This means the husband's rule over his wife is a fallen part of creation! It is not a part of God's intention for humanity, but a result of our sinful nature!

The Bible offers an uneven witness because of the culture in which it was written. But today it is critical that we fully embrace women's leadership and the Bible tells us why.

Certainly, because it is just. Since all are made in the image of God, it is categorically prejudicial to bar over half the human race from leadership in the church.

Secondly, it is practical. It is clear today that women are fully capable and, by barring them from certain professions – who knows – maybe it will be a woman that will cure cancer? 1 Corinthians 12:7 tells us that each is given a gift of the spirit for the common good. God gave women these gifts and, without them, society will suffer.

Finally, the Westminster Catechism tells us the chief end of humanity is to glorify God and enjoy God forever. 1 Peter 4:10-13 makes it clear how are to do this,

Whoever speaks, is to do so as one who is speaking the utterances of God... so that in all things God may be glorified through Jesus Christ... As each one has received a special gift, employ it in serving one another as good stewards of the manifold grace of God.

That was my mother's calling. To be a good steward of the manifold grace of God. It was in the beginning of women in ministry, but she was unflappable. She never defended herself because it was clear her authority was from God. Rather than argue, she demonstrated the truth through using her gifts and, as a result, converted thousands upon thousands of people over the course of her six decades of ministry...which still continues.

Her call became clearest to others during the time of the bombing in Cambodia in the 1970's. Students were hunkered down in a Hamilton Hall classroom of Columbia University in protest.

But Abigail Rian Evans, as university chaplain, after an all-night prayer vigil with the student Christian fellowship, met with the protesters and brokered a plan for them to leave. Otherwise the university president would not let the long-planned outreach series of events called "Jesus Week" proceed on campus. And so she gathered Episcopalians, Presbyterians, Baptists, Methodists, Campus Crusaders, Intervarsity, Mennonites, and more for an event called "Jesus Week".

Through proclaiming Christ, she helped unify that fractured community. That moment crystalized her call in the eyes of hundreds, perhaps even thousands or tens of thousands, for the story was printed in *Parade Magazine*, written by Ann Proctor. Almost 50 years later, my mother co-authored a book, *Faith of Our Mothers, Living Still: Princeton Seminary Women Redefining Ministry*, and Ann Proctor wrote this review:

> *Like the women at Jesus' tomb who were the first to bear witness to his resurrection, the women in "Faith of Our Mothers, Living Still" have dared to step out boldly, despite opposition, and make a difference in their worlds. The good news that Abigail Evans and Katharine Sakenfeld proclaim, in page after page, is that, ordained or not, each of us is called to ministry that can change lives.*

A sinner is justified by grace alone (sola gratia)

through faith alone (sola fide)

for the sake of Christ alone (solus Christus), a truth

revealed to us in Scripture alone (sola Scriptura).

Awkward Verses... Give Up or Drop Dead
Acts 5:1-6

The second chapter of Acts contains the most beautiful and wondrous verses in all the Bible about the church. The goodwill, the generosity, the love, and the devotion to God convey the ideal every church strives for; it is simply glorious.

But only a few chapters later, it begins to fall apart.

The grace and goodwill disintegrate when a couple sells their land and fails to give the proceeds to the church. Peter shames Ananias, who drops dead on the spot. When his wife, Sapphira, appears rather than showing sympathy for her loss, he doubles down on his criticism and she dies as well.

Apparently, Acts is trying to teach us that the church is all about love and forgiveness except when it comes time to tithe. Give up or drop dead is the clearest message that comes through!

Just like the other passages we have studied this month; these verses prove problematic for our faith today. We understand the church to be a place of grace. After all, this faith was founded upon the sacrificial death of Jesus, a supreme act of love. We remember Jesus taught Peter to forgive seventy times seven.

We can also easily cite scores of passages like Second Corinthians 9, that teach we should give voluntarily and not as an extortion... "*each of you must give as you have made up your mind, not reluctantly or under compulsion*". Clearly the threat of death is extortion. So which passage do we follow?

Luke, the author, offers no commentary or insight into this event, leaving us the impression that all that transpired was God's will and that Peter was his agent. It leaves me wondering, and perhaps you too, that if God truly, genuinely works this way, I should be walking around with a lightning rod on my head, for surely, I have committed worse sins than this.

It is also problematic for preachers. We need your tithe to do God's work through the church. Passages like this can be used to not only inflict guilt into your heart, but mortal fear of being smote by the Lord if you don't give enough! This prosperity gospel nonsense not only tries to convince people that if you give generously enough to the church your personal finances will multiply. But the converse that if you fail to give, like Ananias and Sapphira, you will be severely punished.

Yet, it is also all too easy to simply dismiss this passage. We are a church of love and grace and often we are tempted to soft peddle Jesus.

We know that Jesus lived love and grace, but he also believed that to embrace this love meant being willing to give up everything... whether it is your family, your possessions, or your life. In Luke, he tells us,

Whoever does not bear his own cross and come after me cannot be my disciple. So therefore, any one of you who does not renounce all that he has cannot be my disciple.

Because the church has been so maligned (for good reasons and bad) we sometimes lose our courage to preach the demands of the gospel. But all that is left is a milquetoast message of "live and let live".

As a result, we will seek to balance this passage with the grace and forgiveness of our God while discovering the demands this passage places on our lives of faith.

Perhaps the most important point is that, despite our first impression, there is nothing in the text that indicates a harsh penalty from God.

Nowhere in this text are the deaths of Ananias and Sapphira attributed to the power of God or even Peter. It is true Peter shows no sympathy, but neither does he invoke some curse to cause their deaths. This means we are left wondering what caused their deaths. Perhaps it is not too far of a stretch to believe it was extreme shame combined with a bad heart.

But there is also a theological lesson.

Rather than sin leading to divine punishment, sin itself, and its natural consequences, are its own punishment. In Proverbs 8:36 God declares,

All who fail to find me harm themselves; those who hate me love death.

Ananias and Sapphira knew they were becoming a part of this new community in which everyone was entrusting everything to God, but they held something back, which meant they held back on fully giving themselves over to the Lord's protection. They were trusting in God *and their money*. And that's the problem.

It is a delusion that the money in your bank (or anything else in your life for that matter) will offer you something that God cannot. In a very real sense, failing to give according to **your conscience**, not your preachers', not your parents', but yours, is failing to trust in God which is in and of itself death.

Failing to live a life of generosity with your finances, with your time, with your whole being is a recipe for a miserable life!

If the movie *It's a Wonderful Life*'s lead character was Mr. Potter, it is easily could have been titled… *It's a Miserable Life!*

Perhaps even worse than Scrooge in his miserliness, Mr. Potter is the most cantankerous and wretched character ever to grace the big screen. He revels in the misfortune of others and devotes his life to using disasters in others' lives to line his own pockets!

I would wager you know someone like this. Not the caricature that is Mr. Potter, but someone who is so terrified of the future and everyone around them that the only solace they can find is in the bank. And, because of it, they have spiraled into loneliness and despondency.

Ananias and Sapphira died from hearts shriveled by fear. They failed to give to the community and, as a result, others went hungry. We must not; we cannot do the same.

This town has a shocking need. The poverty rate in this city is a horror. The racial disparity is a shame. And you and I have been commanded by God, by our Lord, to go and be generous so that no one goes without.

It is not a sin to be wealthy. It is a blessing from God. But it is a sin to hoard it and to hold on to it.

But you know this already. You know that when you are generous, your heart feels whole. You feel complete. You feel peace knowing you are doing the right thing.

It is summed up in Second Corinthians 9:6,

> *The one who sows sparingly will also reap sparingly... and the one who sows bountifully will also reap bountifully.*

This is not the promise of financial riches but something of infinite more value: the presence of God in your heart.

To be generous, sacrificially generous, is to imitate Christ who gave it all on the cross. To sow generously in the lives of others is to live your purpose for being on this planet.

I have everything, and I mean that. Everything. Everything any reasonable person could want.

A wonderful family. A wonderful home. A fantastic town to live in and a place to go to everyday, filled with beautiful people trying to do their very best for His sake. And since I have everything, it means I owe everything, all of it, every bit of it to God.

First Presbyterian is the same way. As a church we are phenomenally blessed.

And as we look at the challenging story of Ananias and Sapphira, we must ask ourselves... Are we giving as generously and sacrificially as the Lord our God calls us?

Recently, on a Wednesday evening as Kirk Neely was teaching on prayer, a young man challenged us to do just that. Give everything away in order to be faithful to Christ. Literally sell it all!

Pastor Craig was there.

This young man was jogging through our campus and started shouting obscenities at us!

He was cursing us because of the size of our buildings. He said that we should sell the entire campus, everything, and give it to the poor. He said Jesus would be ashamed of us, that Jesus would spit on us, and that we were the worst kind of Christians.

And for just an instant, I thought...maybe we should. But which parts would we sell?

>...Should we sell the Mobile Meals building that feeds 1500 people a day?

…or the Clark Building which cares for children during the week?

…or perhaps the upstairs which houses seniors from the community for friendship, education, and recreation?

…or perhaps the church gym, in which people from over the community come to play basketball?

…maybe some of the offices in which Kirk Neely offers counseling for those in crisis?

…could we get rid of the Columbarium, which serves as a place of solace and comfort for those who have lost loved ones?

…perhaps it should be the Arthur Center, which not only hosts community education events, but is used to distribute meals to the needy four times a month?

So, let our generosity in all things, but especially in our love and grace, be equal to that of our Lord. Amen.

www.ingramcontent.com/pod-product-compliance
Lightning Source LLC
Chambersburg PA
CBHW072019110526
44592CB00012B/1377